THE ECONOMY OF
ENOUGH

UNLOCKING THE SECRET TO HAPPILY EVER AFTER

BRONWEN SCIORTINO

© Copyright Bronwen Sciortino 2018

First Published in 2018 by sheIQ Life Pty Ltd.

All rights reserved. No part of this publication may be reproduced, stored in a retrieval system, or transmitted in any form or by any means, electronic, mechanical, photocopying, recording or otherwise, without the written permission of the publisher.

The Author and Publisher of this book do not make any claim or guarantee for any physical, mental, emotional or spiritual result. All products, services and information provided by the author are for general education and entertainment purposes only. The information provided herein is in no way a substitute for medical or other professional advice. In the event you use any of the information contained in this book for yourself, the author and publisher assume no responsibility for your actions.

Illustrations: Dale Simmonds, Giant Advertising
www.giantadvertising.com.au

Cover Design: Book Baby LLC
www.bookbaby.com

Typesetting: Kelsey Allen, Media Highway
www.mediahighway.com.au

Edited by Jessica Zaccaria

ISBN: 978-0-9943188-3-1
ePUB version: 978-0-9943188-4-8
PDF – Merchant version: 978-0-9943188-5-5

Sciortino, Bronwen

The Economy of Enough (Unlocking the Secret to Happily Ever After)

ABOUT THE AUTHOR

Bronwen Sciortino is an internationally renowned Author, Simplicity Expert and Professional Speaker who spent almost two decades as a high-powered, award-winning executive before experiencing a life-changing event that forced her to stop and ask the question "What if there's a better way to live?"

Based in Perth, Western Australia, Bronwen works with people globally through corporate programs, conference platforms, retreats, professional mentoring and in the online environment. She shares her secrets to success and inspires individuals to simplify their lives and embrace the concept of an economy of enough.

Bronwen blogs regularly for global platforms, has been featured in 'The Book of Amazing People', 'Reboot Your Life – Phoenix Edition', and 'Successful Women in Business Winners Edition', and is regularly invited as a guest interviewee on blogs, podcasts and member sites situated throughout the world.

In her spare time you'll find her on her yoga mat, immersed in the world of meditation, curled up with a great book or exploring the great outdoors.

DEDICATION

This book is for you – the one who knows what it feels like to desperately wish you could lift the weight of the world from your shoulders.

The time for slogging has passed – the time for being happy is here.

May these pages guide you to your happily ever after with love, ease and grace.

Much love

Bron xo

Contents

CHAPTER 1	INTRODUCTION	1
CHAPTER 2	SEEKING SALVATION	6
CHAPTER 3	GREAT EXPECTATIONS	17
CHAPTER 4	ALONE	30
CHAPTER 5	GIVING AND TAKING?	42
CHAPTER 6	PLAYING THE GAME	53
CHAPTER 7	FEAR OF MISSING OUT (FOMO)	66
CHAPTER 8	SOLDIER ON	77
CHAPTER 9	LIVE AND LET LIVE	89
CHAPTER 10	ENERGY RULES	102
CHAPTER 11	HIDDEN MESSAGES	114
CHAPTER 12	THE OTHER SIDE OF CHANGE	126
CHAPTER 13	FINDING YOU	138
CHAPTER 14	THE ECONOMY OF ENOUGH	149
CHAPTER 15	CONCLUSION	160
	CONTACT DETAILS	164
	REFERENCES	165
	THANK YOU	166

CHAPTER 1

Introduction

There's something extraordinarily powerful that happens when you believe that you are enough. Being 'enough' of something, or to someone, has the power to lift us as high as we can go in our lives … or to bring us to the depth of a deep, dark abyss.

The word 'enough' has a different meaning to everyone, and how you define it will determine your relationship with it and the way you journey through every day. For one individual, their definition of enough money might not even scratch the surface of enough money to another person. There may easily be enough time for one person but nowhere near enough time for another. Enough is fluid, mysterious and, often, all consuming.

If you're like me, then the concept of enough may well have factored as one of the biggest challenges of your life. You're well acquainted with the depths of that abyss, and you most likely haven't experienced the highs that are available to some. You're probably also caught in a never-ending spiral of trying to beat this nemesis; just when you think you've got it beaten, it finds a way to provide you with a comparison that you simply can't live up to. You spend your life trying to measure up against an invisible foe – one that grows stronger every day.

Our relationship with enough is in direct correlation to the lessons we have been taught in our formative years, coupled with the way we have internalised those lessons, and then overlaid by the individual filters we apply. Sounds complicated, right? That's because it is, or rather because we've managed to find a way to make it complicated.

As human beings, we have a unique ability to make everything in our lives complex. We've spent millions, perhaps even billions, of years evolving as a species and we've reached a point where we've created pathways that force us to find more and more complex ways to survive. Otherwise, it feels like we're standing still – and along the way we've learned that standing still can be dangerous.

Our lives spin at incredible speed. We live on the edge of exhaustion and somehow, we've created a way of life that ensures we carry a belief system that keeps us small. We blindly follow anyone and anything around us that offers us a glimmer of hope that there might be a light at the end of the tunnel – an exit to a better way of living. We find ourselves living a way of life that makes us believe that if we aren't stressed and exhausted then we can't be successful. If we miss out on something then we might just miss our calling, our 'download' or our 'golden nugget' that will catapult us to success. We get caught up and engrossed in trying to be and do what others are and have done, because we are grasping for the way to a better life.

What remains for us is a life that is overly busy and filled with often meaningless 'stuff' driving our every decision, action and reaction. Our heads are spinning, our health is declining and we're left with a sense that there is an empty space within us – one that we have no idea how to fill.

We go about our days trying to fit more in, undertake more self-development, constantly refine, grow, develop … and the list goes on. We're driven to make ourselves 'better' people. No matter how hard we try, we simply never measure up and we always end up not being good enough – *by our own measure.*

How do I know all this? Well, because I perfected living this way, pushing myself to the extreme until I collapsed under the weight of my everyday life. I experienced a crash of such significance that I was shattered into a million pieces and unable to get back up.

Every traumatic experience is different and completely unique to the individual who experiences it, but I can tell you this: when you find yourself at the absolute bottom of the pit that awaits you after a complete breakdown, there is only one thing that is clear. You are left with two simple choices: to live or to die.

I chose to live.

Having made this choice, I then began the long, hard, confronting and excruciating climb to claw my way back to living.

When you're enmeshed in your life, and you're stuck in a spiral, there is no room to see that anything could be more difficult than what you are experiencing. My experience has left me without any doubt that clawing your way resolutely back from the bottom of the pit is the hardest challenge you will ever have to face – if you ever find yourself there.

And, having experienced the depths and extremes of the pit, I don't ever want to see anyone else find themselves in one. Especially when I now know that there are so many simple and easy things we can do to live our lives in a completely different way.

My journey back to a 'normal' life has convinced me that we've all been hoodwinked, and that there are a number of stories that we've either been told – or that we've been telling ourselves – that force us down a path leading inevitably to our own destruction.

There is another way to live – and I know that it is no more difficult than learning to ask yourself a few simple questions. I know this because I now live very differently every day and it's those questions that keep me on an even keel.

I wrote this book as a way to share with you some of the things I've learned through recovering from a total breakdown and journeying back to a different way of life. It's my hope that you can take some of these lessons and find your own path for your *own* life.

Every time I speak to an audience – no matter how large or small, no matter where in the world that audience is located – I am often asked a question about how to get started on the journey of living your life differently.

My answer to this question is always this: you are the only person in your life who knows *your* answers. To make the start point easier for you, I've included a section at the end of every chapter that provides you with some things to think about, ask yourself or do, so that you can create simple and practical steps that are easy to implement, and that can help to take your life in a different direction.

For those of you who've read my previous book, <u>*"Keep It Super Simple – Tips from a Recovering Perfectionist"*</u> you'll know that I combined **'simplicity'** and **'wisdom'** to create the **'KISSdoms'** that were included at the end of each of its chapters. This time I have combined **'enough'** with **'wisdom'** so that they could become **'NUFFdoms'**.

The NUFFdoms will show you that making change easily is as simple as making a choice to do things differently. Your journey doesn't have to be hard, and you don't have to wait; you can start right now. These easy and practical steps can set your life on a brand-new course, allow you to take a few new turns and experience your life in a way that's more aligned with who you really are.

Every book carries a hope for the world. May this book open your heart to the greatness you carry and soothe your soul, so that you may see that you don't need to fear change, you no longer need to look outside yourself for your answers and that living life in a different way is not only easy but it can be loads of fun!

CHAPTER 2

"...like the rest of us he seeks an external saviour."

Philip K. Dick

Seeking Salvation

For at least twelve months before my world shattered, I remember repeatedly thinking that it must be easier to go and spend some time in a mental health clinic, doped into oblivion on drugs and sitting around doing nothing all day rather than keep on showing up for my everyday life. I was under so much pressure and had reached such a level of extreme exhaustion that it is hard to remember how I got myself out of bed, let alone kept on going. But somehow I artificially manufactured the strength to keep pushing myself forwards.

There is no greater evidence of the strength and power of my mind than this sheer fact alone. If only I had an inkling as to the ways that strength and power could have been used for the positive – to propel me in an entirely different direction.

I had so completely lost confidence in myself and my self-esteem was at such a low that I didn't even realise that I was no longer engaged in a battle to try and be good enough. Instead, I had simply capitulated to the point where I was overwhelmed by the sensation of failing at every turn.

Even though I forced myself forward, often through sheer will alone, in my heart I was desperate for a way out – almost to the point of handing over all decision-making authority to a complete stranger who could artificially create oblivion for me through medical intervention.

I was so desperately trying to appear perfect that I let my pride dictate to me what I was and wasn't prepared to do in my life. I was stressed, exhausted, overwhelmed and seriously unwell, and I hid it all from myself whilst pretending that everything was perfect and trying to show that life was one success after another.

In my drive to keep myself small, I had to lessen who I was as a person. The most efficient way for me to do this was to create an alternate reality for myself where I struggled constantly with not being 'enough'. I had been taught that show-offs aren't liked or accepted in so many different aspects of my life and, already feeling like an outsider, I was determined not to do anything else that would ostracise me even further.

I had fallen into the trap of becoming resigned, and I completely bought into the belief that you accept your lot in life with gratitude because after all, there is always someone else who is worse off than you are.

Resignation is as powerful as hatred and bitterness; they all succeed in wearing you down and holding you in place while the world moves on around you.

The reality was that I was desperately seeking salvation from my life, but I was too busy admonishing myself for all the ways that I had failed to understand that there was a path away from where my life was heading.

Having now survived my own Armageddon, understanding that it was *completely self-architected*, and of course with the value that hindsight always adds, I can now clearly see all the signs that were telling me, warning me, and eventually *screaming* at me to stop.

I powered through them all.

The thing about this that I now find the most fascinating is that there is not one single thing that I have in my life now that wasn't readily, easily and affordably available to me *before* I hit the wall. I was so wrapped up in my war against enough that I couldn't see past the horrible and nasty things the voice in my head was saying. The bigger the battle became, the more intense and powerful the voice.

Pride is usually second only to ego, and even though I didn't believe that I was egotistical, that was only because I had adopted an extreme definition of what that was. I used to believe that being egotistical meant that you had a very high opinion of yourself, you weren't shy in telling the world exactly how good you thought you were, and that you were 'up yourself'.

Most young children are pulled into line at some point in their young years and told that *'nobody likes a show-off'* and that *'only nice young children'* are liked by other people. I was no exception to having been told this, but I took the message one step further and internalised it so strongly that it drove me to keep myself small – so much so that I made sure that I did everything I could to be liked by those around me. Even though I mastered the 'playing small' aspect and I kept myself hidden under the radar most of the time, I didn't ever really feel like I belonged anywhere. I spent decades squashing myself into the smallest version of myself so that no one around me would be impacted by me in any way.

It wasn't until I learned that there was another way to view ego, and that it might be a more powerful way for me to move forward, that I gained some clarity around the way that my definition of ego had been holding me back.

The reality is that we all have an ego.
A further reality is that having an ego is not a bad thing.

Dictionary.com tells us that the ego is the *'... I or self of any person; a person as thinking, feeling and willing, and distinguishing itself from the selves of others and from objects of its thought'*.

Being able to look at ego from a different perspective, I can now see that my ego is simply my sense of self. Furthermore, I now see that the challenge I have had with my ego is in no way related to allowing myself to be who I am. Rather, it's about being able to stand strongly in my own shoes and stay true to who I am, no matter what is going on in the world around me.

As I started to learn more about ego and the role that it plays in our lives, I started to make it a priority for me to be able to identify when I was triggered by something or someone. Or when I was acting, reacting or behaving in a way that was not true to who I am. I learned how to be able to gently and compassionately bring myself back to centre.

The more I learned, the more I came to understand the importance of tempering ego with self-compassion. I had decades of conditioning that needed to be undone – regarding how I viewed ego, and the way that I would harshly punish myself if I felt my ego was out of check. It became critical to find a gentle and simple way for me to undo this toxic conditioning.

For almost all of my life I had been very sensitive to other people's opinions. So, my ego had been locked in a box and harshly shut down if it should cause me to act in a way that threatened my ability to hide under the radar. Unwinding this meant that I had to learn to allow my ego to breathe, for it to be allowed out into the world and for it to be allowed to shine in its own right.

The more I learned about myself and allowed myself to stand in the world on my own terms, the more my ego could freely ebb and flow through every day. I started to be able to hand back other people's 'stuff' to them and not be swayed by the emotions that came with it. It became about being able to look honestly at a situation and be confident that I would be able to remain true to who I am at all times.

I also started to allow myself to be open to learning about all sorts of new and different things, in places and from people that I was previously closed off to; my old behaviours made sure I was intent on never stepping out of line.

Some of these lessons have come from highly spiritually evolved people, and from exploring and experiencing spiritual teachings that I was previously blind to. From these teachings, I've learned to apply a spiritual context to the ego as well. When I learned to expand my

awareness of my ego and to accept and love it, I was better able to understand who I am. It has also enabled me to let go of judgement of others, because I understand that any judgement I make is based on only a sliver of information I possess about them, and that the judgement is likely full of my own assumptions anyway. In addition, I can now clearly see that the less time I spend worrying about someone or something else, the more energy I have to put into the things I am passionate about.

I've learned to apply a curiosity to my life that allows me to explore where my mind goes. I used to shy away from knowing any of my own answers, because they might reveal something too painful – like things that needed fixing, or things that might just make me bad or evil. There was so much pain associated with this that it became too difficult for me to look within; there was too much 'stuff' shoved down into deep, dark corners because it had been deemed unacceptable by others.

Having picked up and looked at every shattered piece of myself when I was broken on the floor, and smothering them with self-compassion, I can now look at all of myself – including all the pieces that were hidden in those deep, dark corners – and know that there is nothing there that isn't fit for the world to see.

The reality of life is that if you don't do some things differently, at least some of the time, then you will end up experiencing life in exactly the same way. My journey has taught me that there's nothing wrong with standing still; it's a great thing to do at different times in your life, and indeed is a fabulous skill to master. Knowing when to stand still, when to step gently and when to surge in your life is an art and one that I believe all of us could benefit from knowing.

Learning to ask yourself questions, answer them *honestly* and then gently explore the answers will allow you to be conscious about the decisions you are making in your life. I also know how critical it is to understand that by making no changes to your life, you are *choosing to live your life the way that you are living it now*. You might be able to come up with a thousand reasons why you have to do what you do, live how you live and suffer the life that is yours, but make no mistake: it is your choices that hold you in place and allow you to hide behind the distractions you have created for yourself.

I know this is a confronting thought to consider; I used to be where you are. I can also tell you that gaining an understanding of your ego, setting it free to ebb and flow through your life, bringing yourself back to centre and truly understanding who you are is one of the strongest places to be. There is very little in life that impacts you if you can just get yourself to the other side of fear and distraction.

By creating a gentle and compassionate exploration process, I have enabled myself to ask any question and simply let the answer stand. There is no longer a need for justification or judgement of any of my answers because I know that whatever the answer to a question is, it simply leads me to another question. Each question builds a framework to provide me with information, and the information I gather allows me to make conscious decisions about where my next step might be. This process is my way of seeking salvation *for myself*.

Using this process allows me to find my own answers and, most importantly, learn from myself. The more I understand and love my ego, the more aware I become of how I act, react, think and behave. I know myself, inside and out, and I know that I am worthy of shining. I know who I am, and that is the most empowering place to stand.

NUFFdoms

Most of us are taught to be a small version of ourselves at some point in our life. Whether it's the role that we play in our family unit, a work environment that teaches us there's something about ourselves that isn't acceptable or even a team environment where we feel like we have to be someone we're not to fit in, situations can and do arise where others expect us to be someone we're not.

For all sorts of reasons, we convince ourselves that we have to stay put in these places.

When you finally realise that being asked to be someone or something that isn't aligned with who you are is a beautiful sign that you're meant to be doing something else, you'll suddenly see that there's a different way for you to live.

To help you get there a little more seamlessly, try asking yourself these questions:

1. Think about a situation in your life where someone has asked you to do something that you really don't want to do (but for whatever reason you ended up doing anyway). Write down what this situation was, and how you felt to be involved in something that you didn't want to be doing:

   _____

   _____

   _____

2. Thinking about the decision making process you used to get involved in the situation listed in question 1, would you say that you made a conscious or unconscious decision to get involved?

   _____

   _____

3. While you were involved in the situation (or are involved if you're still there!), did you feel energised or drained whilst involved?

_____
_____
_____

4. Would the activity or situation be something you would actively seek out yourself if someone hadn't asked you to be involved?

_____
_____
_____

5. If you had the opportunity to stop doing the activity or being involved in the situation right now –with no repurcussions – would your answer be 'Yes'? (leave all the reasons and defences about 'why' you have to stay there aside for just a minute and keep this question and its answer really simple):

_____
_____
_____

6. If your answer to question 5 is 'Yes' write down three simple things you can do to help you remove yourself from this activity or situation:

1. _____
_____

2. _____
_____

3. _____
_____

7. Write down when and how you will start to implement step 1 listed in question 6:

_____

_____

_____

_____

Notes

CHAPTER 3

"...and it was not until I began to think, that I began fully to know how wrecked I was, and how the ship in which I had sailed was gone to pieces."

Charles Dickens, Great Expectations

Great Expectations

Often, it's not until you crash and burn that you feel the crippling weight that you've been carrying, day in and day out, for a very long period of time. As with all things that have weight to them, the longer you hold onto it, the heavier it becomes. The only variable is your ability to use your mind to generate the strength you need to help you counter the weight that you are carrying.

As we grow, we start to interact with the world. The people around us start to judge our abilities and then create plans for where we should end up in the greater scheme of life. We're assessed in all sorts of ways – intellectually, physically (coordination, speed, endurance and the like), socially and creatively. Then we're pigeon-holed and funnelled into the different places that other people deem right for us.

Remember back in primary school, when the teacher asks the students what they want to be when they grow up? The options are plentiful, and there's excitement, hope and anticipation, but also control. I remember hearing Australian mountaineer, Michael Groom, present at a conference many years ago and he mentioned that this had happened in his own youth. However, instead of having dreams of being a fireman or a doctor, he was adamant that he wanted to be a mountaineer. He was convinced that someday he'd conquer Mount Everest. But instead of encouragement and support, he was ridiculed by his classmates and his teacher. In fact, his teacher actively led the class in laughing at his ambition. In that moment, he was faced with either making himself small and accepting the expectations of others or choosing to do what he truly desired, despite opinions to the contrary.

Most of us have experienced something similar to this, and our self-worth and ability to achieve our dreams takes a serious hit.

Right then, in that moment, our direction in life is challenged and can significantly impact some of the first steps we take towards our future. Sadly, the vast majority of us choose to shrink back away from the criticism and blend back into the mainstream expectations of who we are, and what our options for our future *should* be.

What really happens is that plans are made, discussions are had and seemingly greater minds than our own start plotting the course of our lives. We're supported and channelled in the directions that others see as the best fit for us. At some point we pop our heads above the parapet and say: *'I'd like to try this'*. Then we are judged as either being worthy, or we're told that we really need to focus in a different direction.

We allow ourselves to be shaped and moulded by the people around us and, simultaneously, we allow their expectations of us to settle on our shoulders, becoming the mantle that we will carry for as long as we remain unconscious to its presence.

Our minds are so much more powerful than we will most likely ever know. And yet, most of us are so successfully programmed from such a young age that the power within us goes completely untapped for most of our lives.

The more I pondered this during my recovery, the more I wondered: why, if our minds are truly that powerful, do we allow ourselves to be led around by the nose like a prize bull in a show ring? For that matter, why does a bull, with all its power and muscle, allow itself to be led around a show ring? Why do we need to be led? Why do some people feel the need to do the leading? Why are there so many situations in life where there is one person that has to be above another? Why do we feel like we have to prove so many things to so many others around us if we dare to step outside the ring that has been created for us?

I found that the more I asked these questions, the more confused the answers became. I couldn't make any sense from the way that all of this was structured. It felt dark and cloying, like it would smother me if I couldn't break free.

When the solution struck me, it was like a lightning bolt from the sky. I realised that I was asking questions that kept me locked within the construct of the expectations that other people had created for me. The answers felt so cloying because they were questioning the very fabric of my existence. The fact that I was even asking the questions was challenging all the programming that had taught me to stay within my defined groove.

When my world was shattered, the fabric that had kept me held in such a tight grasp was ripped forever, and for the first time I was consciously aware that I was seeing a glimpse of the opportunity that awaited me on the other side of great expectations.

I can only describe this sensation almost like being able to look at the world through eyes other than my own. International best-selling author, Wayne Dyer, was fond of saying: 'when you change the way you look at things, the things you look at change' and for the first time I could completely understand what he meant.

I realised that I had unconsciously placed myself in situations throughout my life that forced me to take steps in directions that weren't right for me. I studied subjects at school and university that I didn't really like. I began a career in the corporate world in an industry that was of no interest to me, yet I stayed there for almost two decades.

Because of these choices, I allowed myself to constantly be surrounded by people whose opinions of what I should do, where I should go and how I should progress my career provided me with advice that only sought to keep me more lost.

Just like most people I started looking around for examples of success, so that I might be able to copy their path and find a short cut to my *own* success. However, this served only to amplify the expectations of others and increase the load I was carrying.

At the same time, I became so locked into the game of perfection that I was heaping additional expectations on myself, all the while trying to find who I was whilst walking in the dark.

> *I was my own harshest critic and I had created such extreme expectations of myself that I had stacked my own game of life against me.*

I had no idea of the additional load that I had heaped on top of the expectations of others – nor how free I would feel when that load was lifted.

I used to be ruled by the clock. The alarm would go off in the morning, demanding my presence in the day. I'd rush through the morning routine, with everything being done in order so that nothing was missed out. I arrived at the office at almost the same time every morning, at which point my diary ran my entire existence: it ruled where I was, what was being done and the timeframe within which I had to do it. Then, work appointments governed where I was and when I had to be there. Finally, I was able to head home, cook dinner and then spend time working on all of the things that didn't get done during the day. I'd head to bed, and then the cycle began again.

Everything was driven in relation to time. Because I was so conscious of time ticking away, I was very respectful of other people's time. I was always at least five minutes early for a meeting or appointment with someone else, because I understood the impact of creating additional time pressure.

Time was actually my nemesis; there was always more to get done than time would allow. I became a proponent of the concept of needing another day in the week. I had no idea that living in this construct simply added weight to the delivery of expectations – that allowing time to create pressure was literally adding to the weight my life had become.

I didn't know it, but the load that time had created lifted in the instant that my world shattered around me. I suddenly found myself in a space that seemed to have no time. The world continued on around me with everyone carrying on their everyday lives, but for me time ceased to have any meaning.

People were talking to me, but it seemed like their words were coming from a long way away. The days still rolled over but they had no relevance in my world. The clock still ticked away its minutes and hours, but it no longer had any influence over what happened in my days.

> *Time ceased to play a significant role in my life, and suddenly the pressure that time applied was no longer present for me.*

I found myself in a place where there was nothing but time – and I had no idea what to do with it. I had come from a place that was so driven, so structured and so busy that an abundance of time was something I had never experienced before.

It can be very unsettling to find yourself in an unfamiliar place. Looking back on it, I think that because everything in my life was uprooted all at once, there was nothing in my tool kit that could help me to see that being in a space where time is a leisure is an absolute gift.

I was challenged in every facet of my life – all at once. It didn't matter which direction I looked, there was nothing but the remains of a once powerfully constructed fortress that had been held up by pillars that were the expectations of others.

In the blink of an eye, the fortress was shattered and I found myself wrecked and with the pieces scattered all around me – but somehow those expectation pillars were still standing. Then I noticed an interesting thing that started to happen: the power of the expectations began to wane and their hold over me lessened. It seemed that without the current that time pressure added, the expectations could not hold their grip on my life.

Each day became about the basics of life and finding a new pathway in a simpler structure. I was broken, and I was very fragile, so I had to bring everything back to scratch for me to be able to get through a moment, let alone a day.

As I gradually became used to a life without the pressure of time, I settled into a pattern that became about rebuilding my health and my overall strength and wellbeing. I could no longer face a lot of the activities that I had previously engaged in because, intuitively, I knew that I needed to create a new structure that was built with my own foundation, rather than one given to me by others.

Of course, there was the pull and the temptation to rebuild on the pillars that others had given me. But the more I learned about myself, the more I understood and, eventually, could clearly see that using the previous foundation would only bring me back to the same situation again.

As I rebuilt my life, I started to consider the different ways that I could walk in my newly created world. As I learned to ask myself questions, I also learned to find *my own* answers.

I liked the way that life flowed without the pressure of time, so I decided to explore how I could bring that into the new world order of things. I started to challenge when and how I did things during the day, and I started to bring the power of my mind into my everyday tasks.

I put my watch aside. It's a beautiful watch and something that I love, but I wasn't ready to allow it to wield its power in my life again. Even now, a few years down the track after my recovery, I still rarely wear it.

I don't have an alarm set and often allow myself to simply wake up when I am ready – and I know the thought of this horrifies a lot of people! Except for when I'm doing really intense spiritual work, I also now easily get eight hours sleep a night, so I can readily wake up early in the morning fully recharged and ready to get into the day. For those times that I do need to be up at a specific time, my husband helps me by either waking me or calling me to bring me back from sleep, because I won't have an alarm clock in the bedroom.

I also stopped wondering whether I could meet – or exceed – the expectations of others. Instead, I started focusing on understanding who *I am* and working towards things that would help me to step into my greatness. It became far more important to me to explore how far I can go in this world than it was to remain boxed and shaped by the opinions of other people.

Having experienced the implosion of everything in my life, and the effort that was required to claw my way back through recovery, I was interested only in what life might be like in a different channel. I had been a master at ignoring the warning signs in my life, and it had clearly not worked for me. So, I decided to become a master at listening and understanding *myself*, so that I could walk in my world in a very different way.

Great expectations used to rule my life and they did nothing but guarantee me a miserable half existence. I sat still for so long, making sure I was small and insignificant in the world. I also experienced and survived the crash that came as a result of living this way. I'm done with dancing to the tune of everyone else's song and I am now completely tuned in to that inner voice that tells me that I was made for more – that there is a very different path for me.

Since I've followed that voice and silenced the chorus of expectations, my life is free. It's vibrant and full of colour. For the first time there is absolutely no question over whether or not I'm worthy to be here. And, as an added bonus, I truly know what happiness is.

NUFFdoms

When we allow the expectations of others to take over the direction our lives take, it can lead us on a path that sees us fulfilling the dreams of others. We can also create a life of intense pressure and chronic stress when we heap great expectations on ourselves.

I found that understanding who I AM was a great place to start so that I could better find the things that resonated with my life. Being able to succinctly write down all the things that you are, that you stand for and that are important to you gives you a great guide to use when looking at what you're doing and whether it is in alignment with who you are.

1. Take some time to write down all the things that are true about you. What do you stand for? What's important to you? Use the spokes on the diagram below to write your answers – when you run out of spokes, add some more! Remember – this is purely for you – no one else has to see it – and you don't have to defend the answers to anyone else – just let yourself write whatever comes to mind.

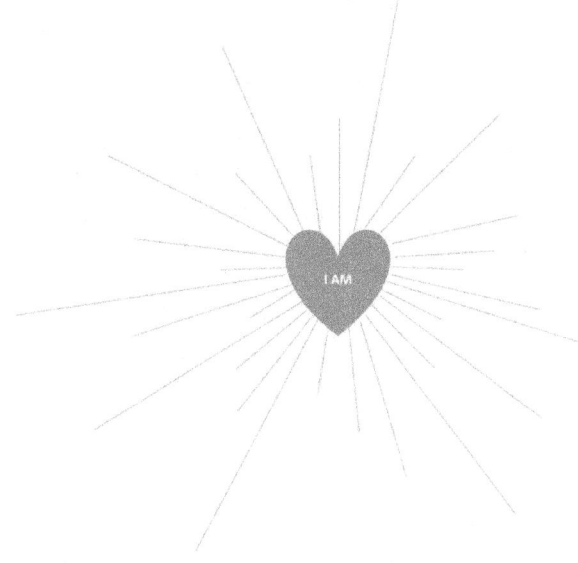

2. Pick something you feel is expected of you in your life by someone around you. Write the expectation down using the space provided below:

_____
_____
_____
_____
_____

3. Using your I AM's that you wrote in the diagram above, write down all the I AM characteristics that the expectation helps you to meet:

_____
_____
_____
_____
_____

4. Using your I AM's that you wrote in the diagram above, write down all the I AM characteristics that conflict with, or are impacted by the expectation that you wrote above:

_____
_____
_____
_____
_____

5. Look at the answers to question 4. Write down how it makes you feel to have your I AM's in conflict with, or impacted by this expectation:

_____
_____
_____
_____
_____

6. Ask yourself whether there is something you can do a little bit differently that would allow you to reduce the impact of this expectation on your I AM's:

_____
_____
_____
_____
_____

7. Write down one step you can take, AND WHEN YOU ARE GOING TO TAKE IT, to start doing this one thing:

_____
_____
_____
_____
_____

Notes

CHAPTER 4

'I felt very still and empty, the way the eye of a tornado must feel, moving dully along in the middle of the surrounding hullabaloo'

Sylvia Plath, The Bell Jar

Alone

There's an emptiness to life when you realise that you are surrounded by people, but you don't fit in. It hits you in the heart and it *burns*. Then you get a sinking sensation in your stomach that morphs into a thought you might not be *good enough* to be accepted. All of this happens in the space of seconds, and suddenly you're well on your way to believing that you need to change yourself before you are able to be accepted.

It's hard to come away from a gathering of friends and feel like everyone else had a great time but you're exhausted from trying to connect. To me, it seemed that hanging with a group came so naturally for everyone else; after all, they have loads to talk about and there's a sense of comradeship and friendship that I never felt was entirely extended to me. Many times, I was left wondering whether it might have been easier to leave me on my own and not invite me anywhere. Most times, I felt like I was on the periphery of life, like an optional extra – almost like the sauce that you can choose to have with your fries.

It feels like I've existed on the edge of other people's lives, putting a toe in the water and feeling like a failure because I couldn't quite work out how to change myself so that I would fit in. If I was invited somewhere I would force myself to go, with an uneasy feeling in my stomach about whether I could blend in enough so as to not put anyone out. Mentally, I would squash myself into the smallest version of me so that the world around me wasn't impacted by my presence.

Living like this pushed me to be stronger and being stronger meant that I became a chameleon. Always changing and adapting to my surroundings so that I was camouflaged and rarely ever seen by others around me. What I now know about this strength is that I simply became more accomplished at hiding away from the world. The unintended consequence of mastering chameleonesque abilities was that the longer I forced myself into these situations, the more I lost sight of who I truly was.

To put this into perspective, I spent decades channelling my strength into making sure that I was constantly fading into the background, never outshining or overpowering anyone around me. In fact, I was constantly excelling and overachieving, but always in a way that meant I stood behind someone else.

If I played a brilliant game of netball, I would hide it behind the performance of the team, or by saying *'there's still loads of work to be done'*. If I won an award, I would hide it by not telling anyone, or saying that *'it was only won because of the support of my team'*. Undoubtedly, the team around me contributed to overall successes, but there was not one minute in my life that I personally acknowledged as being special due to the unique and brilliant talents that I brought to the world.

Chameleons aren't supposed to shine; they keep themselves small and hidden away. Somehow, I managed to rise almost to the pinnacle of my previous career – but always one step behind someone else so that I would constantly have a reminder to keep myself just small enough to not overshadow the person at the top.

Living this way is exhausting.

It takes an enormous amount of energy to continuously remember who you 're supposed to be, to whom and in which circumstances.

Although I perfected living this way for a significant period of time, the resultant breakdown should not really have been a surprise.

If I felt like I was alone previously, then hitting rock bottom was perhaps the loneliest place I have ever been, because I didn't even have *myself* for company. I no longer knew who I was; I looked in the mirror and I couldn't look into my own eyes because it terrified me not knowing who was looking back at me. People around me were asking me questions, and my brain couldn't process what they were asking me, let alone coming up with an answer. It felt like there were all these expectations of me and I couldn't live up to any of them.

I had previously numbed the pain of not fitting in by steeling my heart and pushing on through, but when you experience a breakdown it's like being shattered into a million pieces on the floor around you. There are so many pieces, each and every one of them raw and painful, each of them screaming at you for attention. In that moment, it felt like everything I had known, every plan I had in place for my future and every façade I had created for my protection had disintegrated.

When I was at the bottom of the pit that was my breakdown, I was faced with a choice – a choice that in its simplicity asked me to decide whether I wanted to live or to die. I made my choice, and in choosing to live, I chose the long, hard and confronting road to recovery – the road to finding myself.

My journey back to me taught me that I am absolutely, completely and wholly different – and that's exactly the way it's supposed to be. The freedom I felt when I acknowledged this was like nothing I had ever experienced.

By squashing myself into a tiny, camouflaged box, I created a situation where all I wanted was to combat the overwhelming loneliness I was feeling and find a connection with the world. But it wasn't until much later on that I fully understood a life-changing message: trying to fit in with others was never going to give me the connection that I craved. That connection comes only when you align within yourself – an alignment to who you truly are.

For me, connection now comes from spending time with the things, people and places that align with my values and feed the passion in my soul. I know what's important to me and I know the things that fuel my energy – and it's these things that I seek out on a daily basis.

I also now understand that the connection I craved so deeply was actually a hankering for wisdom, and that I was searching for this wisdom in all the wrong places. Deep down, I knew that the way I was living my life wasn't working for me, but I was stuck in the belief that I should suck it up because there were plenty of others whose lives were way worse than mine. I made matters worse for myself by adding another layer of 'requirement': the ingrained thought process telling me that I had so much in my life to be grateful for, and that wanting something other than my 'lot in life' was simply selfish.

It's no wonder my life was empty – *I was empty*. I dragged myself out of bed every day so that I could participate in a bland, stressed and exhausted existence, and then told myself that it would all be OK if I could just get through the latest crisis.

In my very little spare time, I searched fruitlessly for a solution to my life – a solution that would come wrapped in a nice little package that would be acceptable to the world and that wouldn't make me look narcissistic or selfish for wanting something other than what I had.

With the improvements in technology, my search became global. With the help of the internet I was able to access all sorts of information from all kinds of amazing people and places around the world. None of it came wrapped the way I needed it to be, but the reality is that none of it could come wrapped that way. I was too trapped in my fear of failing for any of the information to have been a realistic solution.

So, I soldiered on – while hosting a raging internal battle between my fear of someone finding out that I wasn't perfect and my soul demanding to be released to a life more aligned. This led me even further down the path of exhaustion and feeling like I was letting people down.

The more exhausted I became, the more I gave of myself so that I wouldn't let anyone down. The more I gave, the more I chastised myself for not being strong enough. The harder I tried to be a stronger person, the more I believed that I wasn't organised enough. So, I would push even harder – and give even more – as a form of punishment.

The more I punished myself, the less I believed in the wisdom and knowledge that was uniquely mine to share. The less I believed in myself, the more I tried to change, and the more I tried to change myself, the more lost and alone I became.

Thus, my life became an exhausting and all-consuming spiral that was hidden to the world by a very convincing façade... until it all fell apart.

Through my recovery, I spent years looking at the shattered pieces of myself, because I needed to understand which pieces would help me to live my life differently post-breakdown. In the early days, it was like looking at the pieces of a jigsaw puzzle all jumbled together in the box, with all the important corner and edge pieces hidden amongst the multitude of other pieces, in a riotous jumble of colour and shapes. When I at last understood that each piece served its own unique purpose, the corner and edge pieces of my new way of living life slowly revealed themselves and I was finally able to start building the picture of what my life could look like.

The sense of loneliness in this task was at times crippling and there were days when I would be completely immersed in the emotion of the pieces I was looking at.

I found a pathway through the intensity of this task when I found the way to drop the judgements of my shattered pieces. When I was able to drop the judgement, I was able to disconnect the emotional entanglement that was attached. Without the emotion, the shattered pieces were no longer hidden behind a curtain packed with 'stuff'; rather, they were simply a piece I could choose to put into my picture of life – or not.

For perhaps the first time in my life, I had found a sense of peace and a feeling of calm in being with myself. I finally understood that in my effort to continually present a successful façade, I had given everything I had to everyone else without allowing myself to receive anything in return. I also came to the realisation that if I wanted things to be different moving forwards then I needed to change the way I was living my life.

When you experience a breakdown with the force and magnitude of mine, there are multiple, significant lessons that you learn on your road to recovery. One of the greatest gifts that my recovery gave me was the ability to know who I am again.

All around me – in fact, all around *us* – there are generous and supportive systems that provide us with exactly what we need, when we need it. Every time I have a new realisation, there are suddenly lots of references and information about that thing available to me. In short, we all have exactly what we need, exactly when we need it.

One of the biggest lessons I learned through my journey back to me was the importance of being open to receiving that perfectly timed information – this means being able to switch on your awareness exactly when and where it's needed.

If there is one thing I have deliberately worked to develop through my recovery process, it is the ability to connect to my intuition. I now know, really quickly, when patterns are showing up in my life and I know when they are teaching me to stop, take notice and learn. I can identify within minutes the things around me that are aligned to who I am, and the ways in which those things can, and do, support me in my path forwards.

I know how much it hurt to feel like I never really fit in anywhere, and what it is like to have people all around but constantly feel alone. When I made the choice to live, I was also determined that my life moving forwards would be different.

Coming from ground zero, I had to slog my guts out to do the work that needed to be done. I faced my demons and did the work that enabled me to find my way towards knowing who I am. I had decades of 'stuff' and conditioning to undo, but I was determined to create a different version of myself – one that had way more respect for the gifts and wisdom that I bring to the world, and loads of love and compassion for the honest, generous and loving soul that I am.

Each and every one of these things lessens the hold that 'enough' has on my life. Each time I take a step in the new direction of my life, I take one more step away from the power that I allowed not being good enough to have, and I turn towards honouring my divine pathway in this lifetime.

NUFFdoms

When we push ourselves to the brink, we create a souless life. We empty ourselves of the things that make us special and we're left with a gaping hole and no idea which way to turn to start filling it. We drag ourselves out of bed so that we can exist in life, and then we tell ourselves that it will all be OK if we just push ourselves forwards.

It's time to lay the corner of your own jigsaw puzzle so that you can turn your life in a slightly different direction and start to build a life that you really want to be living. The basis of the following exercise was given to me by my dear friend Anna. She learned it in a different form from Aleksey Phabov who is the founder of the Self Development Centre Arcanum.

1. Take a few moments to write down all the things that are good about the way you are living your life now. Don't think about it too much, simply ask yourself what's great about your life and then write down the words that flow:

   _____
   _____
   _____
   _____
   _____
   _____
   _____
   _____
   _____
   _____
   _____
   _____

2. Now take a few moments to write down all the things that are bad about the way you are living your life now. Don't think about it too much, simply write down the words that flow:

_____

_____

_____

_____

_____

_____

_____

_____

_____

3. Take a few moments to have a look at your answers. The words you've written down will give you a really good idea about the basis of the beliefs you hold around the things you have in your life.

   Start by choosing one of the things you have listed as being bad about the way you are living your life. Take a moment to write down a few things about how this impacts your life and how important you feel it is that this thing change:

   _____

   _____

   _____

   _____

   _____

   _____

4. If you have decided that it is important to change the thing listed in question 3, write down one thing you could do differently to help you change this thing:

_____

_____

_____

5. Write down when you are going to take the first step to make this change happen:

_____

_____

_____

Repeat this process for the items listed on the 'bad' list.

Notes

CHAPTER 5

"You've discovered a wellspring, simply allow it to flow and it will fill your world. Don't try to keep a safe distance so as to see what happens. Don't wait to be certain before you take a step. What you give, you will receive, although it might sometimes come from the place you least expect."

– Paulo Coelho

Giving and Taking

We often talk about things being either good enough or not good enough, but what is 'enough'?

Something I realised during my recovery, as I was trying to unravel the mess that my life had become, was that I had never actually defined what 'enough' was. And yet my life had been ruled by the fact that nothing I achieved or did was ever good enough. Having never defined it, it became almost impossible for me to achieve it. I'd created a nice little conundrum for myself!

No wonder my life was complex and out of control; the construct holding it together was flawed from the start.

To be able to piece myself back together and move my life forward in a different way, I had to find another way to view how I did things – a kinder and gentler way for me to live with the outcomes of whatever I did.

'Enough' is a concept whose shadow spans the entirety of your life. It can be applied to everything you do and can be seen everywhere you go. To try and define it as such an expansive concept was too

overwhelming for me in the early stages of my recovery, so I picked up small pieces at a time and worked out how to apply a new paradigm to each and every one of them.

Because 'enough' had held such an invasive hold on every corner of my life, I decided that it would be better for me to take a different track with the way I wanted my life to be moving forwards.

The first place I turned my attention to was to the way that I talked to myself. I realised that I really wasn't a very good friend to myself, and that I held very different standards for me than I did for anyone else around me. For some reason, I expected a great deal more of myself than I did of anyone else.

If someone around me had a problem, or was struggling with something, I was there to help. If someone was lacking in self-confidence, needed a boost in their self-esteem or wanted to find a way that they could improve themselves or their lives, I was there for them. I was often the first responder for those people, throwing love and support to them and creating opportunities for them to thrive.

But whenever any of those things happened in *my* life, I became harsh and critical of my circumstances. I punished myself relentlessly, with an overarching theme of *'surely I should have that sorted out by now'*.

My journey gifted me with the realisation that punishment had been the underlying message running beneath my life for a very long time. I was constantly berating myself for not achieving outcomes that were mostly undefined and frankly, completely unrealistic. Given that way of living had driven me to a breakdown, it was clear to me that I needed to do some things differently to avoid ever having to experience anything similar again. So, I decided to try and apply the same filters to myself that I did for everyone else.

What a revelation! As I began to apply love and grace to myself in different situations, I noticed that I was restoring a balance to the flow of giving and taking in my life. Previously, I had given everything I had to everyone and taken nothing in return. The flow of energy in my life reflected this cycle, with every inch given over to doing everything for everyone else and very little being done for myself.

Perhaps the clearest indication of this was when I was first diagnosed with a cancerous tumour on my head. My reaction to the diagnosis was pure *annoyance*. Perhaps it would have been kinder for me to have taken some time to step back and work out ways that I could have given more to myself and supported myself through this situation. Instead, I stepped in the opposite direction and only allowed myself half a day to undergo a surgery that was to see a six-centimetre chunk of my head cut out.

Looking back at the different scenarios in my life, my ultimate discovery was that I didn't believe that I was worthy of receiving my own attention. My needs rarely saw the light of day because my focus was on serving the needs of others. And at the very centre of the issue was the fact that I didn't believe that I deserved to be happy.

This morphed into an inability to stand up for myself in any way, and an over-developed ability to stand up for everyone around me. If there was an issue that was impacting me, then I would find a way to live with it and shut down the associated emotion, rather than make a scene. If there was something impacting others, then I would become their champion and jump in to save them.

Creating a life with these constructs did nothing but drain my energy constantly. I wasn't getting the things I needed for me to be okay, and I was limiting the growth and development of the people around me by always stepping in and fighting their battles for them. More importantly, I realised that I was using other people's issues as a big fat distraction so that I didn't have to look too deeply at *my* life, and ultimately do the work that *I* needed to do.

To help with creating a new process that would make it easier for me to move my life in a different direction, I found a few questions that I could ask that would give me clarity around the issue I was looking at.

The first of these questions was: *'Is this issue mine?'*

Asking this question immediately allowed me to see whether or not the issue in front of me was mine or belonged to someone else.

If it was someone else's issue, then my next question became: *'Is this something I need to deal with?'*

If the answer was 'no', then I knew that I needed to step back and let the other person handle and process their own 'stuff'. If the answer was 'yes', then I knew that it was okay for me to step in and get involved.

Here's what I found with this process: it was very unusual for the answer to be 'yes' to getting involved if the issue wasn't mine in the first place.

The more I trusted the answers that I got through this process, the more clarity I got in the direction I needed to head in my life. I realised that it isn't my job to make people understand or to take away their pain. It is my job simply to make sure *I* am okay.

This lesson was one that was really important for me to learn. With the level of work that I am now doing in the world, it was imperative that I understand a fundamental part of the work: while it is my passion to show people there's another way to live, it is their choice and their responsibility to decide whether or not they try a few different things for themselves. If I hadn't learnt this lesson when I was keeping myself small, I would have attempted to take away the pain of the world when I stepped out with my work, and that surely would have crushed me further.

The more I moved to create non-negotiable activities for myself – things, places and people that re-energise me on a constant basis – the more I realised that it is critical to give as much to myself as I do to others. Having experienced what it feels like to drain my energy tank completely dry – and just how hard it was to get the tank refuelled – I know intimately that if you don't dedicate time to yourself then you will have nothing left to give to anyone else.

In a lot of ways, I give more to others now than I ever did before. However, the giving is now done in a very different way: instead of giving everything I have and leaving nothing for myself, I now give in a way that allows space for someone else to decide whether or not they want to walk down that path for themselves. I no longer try and take other people's pain away or process their 'stuff' for them, nor do I take on board other people's 'stuff' and spend valuable time worrying about it for them.

I found it important to lessen my grip on what happens in every second of every day. I no longer try to micro-manage what is happening around me. Part of this is because I no longer feel compelled to make sure everyone else is okay, and part of it is because I realised just how much energy it was taking to try and make sure every second was perfect. Above all, I was able to lessen my grip on trying to control everything because I now know who I am.

I now have much greater self-awareness, and I know that the things I now do are completely aligned with the things that are important to me. Because of this, I no longer worry about being exposed by some random person who might be able to prove that I'm not perfect. Being able to surrender the need to control has been one of the biggest releases of stress and exhaustion from my life.

Aligning my life to my values means that I can easily identify the things that do and don't work for me. The more I choose the things that work for me, the easier my life becomes. The easier my life becomes, the more certain I am that the Universe has my back, and this makes it easier for me to surrender control. Not only am I now able to surrender control, but I also don't feel any desire to try and take it back. I am blissfully happy to have handed it back and now I can focus on who I am and what I need to be okay.

Having lived under the unrelenting hold of not being good enough, I found that the best way to lessen the grip of having to control everything was to understand what makes me tick. I needed to understand more about the ways I was reacting and the things I was hiding from so that I could more easily identify the root cause of my need to control everything. Because I was starting from scratch, this was a long and daunting process.

The more I understand this process, the more I know that it's not about when you start, it's the simple act of starting that makes all the difference.

To understand what I was hiding from, I had to find the way to reconnect with my sense of self. Doing this ultimately led me to explore the need for self-compassion.

Having empathy for humanity, and indeed for our planet in general, is a great thing. It enables us to be mindful of the impact we have on others, and to understand that even as one individual in this vast world of ours, what we do can impact the whole.

However, if you don't shine that empathy on yourself and allow yourself to feel the warmth of the love and care that your empathy brings, then you will always be relying on someone else to provide this for you.

When you rely on someone else, it leaves you in the vulnerable position of always looking outside yourself for the love and validation you crave. As soon as you put yourself in this position, you will have handed over responsibility for how you feel on an ongoing basis.

Realising all of this allowed me to move my life forwards. It gave me the space to understand the importance of creating a new paradigm for my life, one where self-compassion became the solid foundation. The flow of my life then became based on a guaranteed outcome: the simple and effective flow of giving and taking. I no longer relied on anyone to receive anything, because I gave myself exactly what I needed, in the exact way I needed it.

All it took was a conscious decision to design my life so that I could consistently give myself a dose of the love and grace that I had previously given away to others.

NUFFdoms

Learning to hand back other people's issues, and even more importantly not take them on board in the first place, is one of the most empowering things you can do for yourself. Try answering these questions to help you to find a way to think and react differently in those situations where you would normally jump in and try to solve other people's "stuff" for them:

1. Think about an issue that you are dealing with at the moment – one that relates to someone else and is something that they are experiencing. Write the issue down here:

   _____

   _____

   _____

   _____

   _____

2. Ask yourself the question: *'Is this issue mine?'*

   You will receive a 'Yes' or 'No' answer in your head - write down whichever answer came into your head first (don't think about whether the answer is right or wrong, just write the first answer down on the page):

   _____

   _____

   _____

   _____

   _____

3. a) If the answer to question 2 is 'Yes', ask the question: *'How can I look at this issue differently?'* Write down your answers below:

_____

_____
_____

b) Ask yourself the question: *How little involvement can I have with this issue?* Write down your answers below:

_____

_____
_____

4. If the answer to question 2 is 'No' ask yourself the question *'Is this issue something I need to deal with?'* Write your 'Yes' or 'No' answer below:

_____

_____
_____

5. If the answer to question 4 is 'No' (and it would be very unusual for it to be 'yes' given it's not your issue) ask yourself the following question: *'How can I best step away from this issue so that the person involved can learn the lessons they need to learn?'* Write your answers below:

_____

_____
_____

The more you trust the answers you get through this process, the easier it will become for you to see the things you need to get involved with and the things that you need to leave alone. Remember that when you let other people sort out their own 'stuff' you are allowing them to learn the lessons they need to learn to fulfil their life purpose.

Notes

CHAPTER 6

"We all want to break our orbits, float like a satellite gone wild in space, run the risk of disintegration. We all want to take our lives in our own hands and hurl them out among the stars."

– David Bottoms

Playing the Game

At times, it can seem like there's a pecking order in life. At first glance it can look like there are boundaries surrounding the things you can do and the things that are just out of reach. These boundaries can appear from all different directions – like social stigmas, community rules, school demands, family restrictions and sometimes even through association with places, events and individuals.

Life becomes something that happens to and around us, and we're lucky if we get glinting moments of calm. Most of the time, though, we're caught racing around trying to keep our feet under ourselves and overdelivering on too many promises, in the desperate hope that one day it will all work out and we'll be successful. There's never enough time, never enough money and never enough people who can help us, and we're often caught feeling like we will be stuck where we are forever because fate has dealt us a cruel hand.

When you get caught in this type of life spiral it can seem like everything is stacked against you. And if you've believed and internalised limiting beliefs from your formative years, then it can seem like you can only get so far in life before everything starts to work against you.

When I first start working with people, one of the most common things they say that they want to work on is this: *'I'm stuck and I don't know how to move forward'*. On the whole, most of us are so turned around by the shaping and morphing that we do to please everyone around us that we don't know which direction is forwards anymore. We find ourselves wandering and directionless, either believing that *'we're stuck with our lot in life'*, or that everything is as it is supposed to be because *'life wasn't meant to be easy'*.

When I found myself on the floor, shattered and unable to get back up again, it was really difficult to know where to turn to fix my situation. My first reaction was to sink back to the floor and allow the overwhelm of the situation to take me over because it all seemed way too hard to contemplate.

This mindset of overwhelm is something I see a lot now. It's almost as if it is our default setting and we've structured our life game, and all the rules within it, to revolve around the overwhelm trigger. It's a mindset that seems to be fuelled by a belief that we live under a head rule of *all* or *nothing* – that is, go big or go home.

Somehow, we've structured our lives such that we must risk everything to move forwards, and this structure means that when things don't work for us we have to change everything in our lives. Otherwise, we accept that we can't change anything and we take our lumps with a smile.

Having had the experience of recovering from a breakdown, I know what it was like to have to start from scratch, to change everything to be able to move forwards. It took everything I had, including every last skerrick of strength within me, to piece myself back together from a state where everything was utterly broken.

I was forced to stop and take notice of where I was at because I had pushed so far beyond my limits that there was no longer any other option available to me. The sheer slog and magnitude of the confronting, overwhelming and daunting work that it took me to recover was by far the hardest thing I have ever had to do.

One of the best things about having had this experience is that I now know just how simple it is to change the rules of your own game so that you can take overwhelm off your playing field. It is such a simple thing to do, yet it is shrouded in a fog that is almost impenetrable to us because we've allowed ourselves to hide behind our excuses for so much of our lives.

The easiest way to describe the playing field is like this:

Imagine that you are standing at one end of a rectangular sports field. At the other end of the field is the season's trophy that you are competing for.

Even though you've never actually seen it, you imagine that the trophy is gold and shiny, and you want it really, really badly.

Between you and the trophy are a number of people, obstacles and objects. It is their job to distract you from getting to the trophy and being able to pick it up. To get to the trophy, you have to successfully complete a number of challenges.

Now imagine that this is the only information you're given, and you have to try to work out how you're going to get to the other end of the field.

The people standing near you on the field start giving you their opinions on how you should go about getting to the trophy, what you should wear, how you need to behave, the best way for you to do things and what the good, bad, appropriate, fair and right way of going about getting the trophy might be.

So, you start to follow their instructions. You change the way you walk, talk, dress, eat and live so that you can do what they have told you to do. You follow their strategy, their instructions, their beliefs and their code of conduct *to the letter* but you can't understand why you aren't moving forwards.

As you go along, you get feedback from these people as to whether or not they think you've done things in the right way. When they tell you you've done something wrong, you adjust what you're doing to meet their demands.

But it's not working. Despite following their directions, you can't seem to navigate yourself in any direction other than sideways or, more often, backwards.

The people around you start to give you new directions to try and get you moving. You come up with some of your own ideas, but because you are locked into getting your directions from others, you have to ask their opinion about your ideas before you can take any action.

Then some of the people from further down the field come over to see what's taking you so long and they start adding their opinion into the mix as well.

Now you're in a situation where there are so many more conflicting opinions, and you have to choose one of them to be able to take your next step. The problem is, you're confused and frozen in time because you don't want to upset anyone around you, and you also can't remember what it's like to make your own decisions. After all, there are multitudes of others who now do that for you.

At this point, you think that you might have taken a wrong turn somewhere, but you aren't sure. You've absolutely no idea how, or when, this occurred and, worst of all, how you're going to get back on track. But you're still conditioned to seek guidance from others, so you turn to the people around you for help.

There are so many people around you giving you their opinions, and the noise makes it hard for you to think for yourself. Your mind is foggy and the crowd around you has also made it really hard for you to see to the other end of the field – you still can't see the trophy that you're competing for.

In fact, it's so crowded you don't even realise that you're no longer on your field any more and that by following other people's directions you've wandered off onto someone else's path.

Then one day, the penny drops and you suddenly look up and realise what's happening. You know that you are utterly lost. You don't have the slightest clue as to where you are, how you got there, or how or what to change to get yourself moving again. You know that something isn't right, and that you need to change some things, but you have no idea where to start and you're overcome by the overwhelming feeling that rises within you.

So, you stay exactly where you are, pushing through and soldiering on – hoping that, if you just get through this thing you're stuck in, everything will be okay.

In life, we get to see things when we're ready to see them. We will remain stuck exactly where we are, obliviously repeating the exact same patterns until we wake up and get clarity around what we're doing and *why* we're doing it.

In short, we will continue playing our life game by other people's rules until we can see that the obstacles, people and things between us and our trophy are simply distractions that we have put in our own way to stop us from getting to the other end of our field.

I was addicted to perfection, with a side serve of not being good enough at every turn. In my mind, I disguised this with strength – I was strong and therefore was given challenges in life because I could endure them.

The Universe grants us glimpses into our lives at exactly the moment we're ready to see them. The more work you do to make yourself ready, the more glimpses you will receive – it's as simple as that.

One of the most liberating moments of my recovery was when I realised that life is a game and that I am the head coach of my own life path. Furthermore, I realised that there are only three rules in the game of life that are fixed:

1. My life will respond to every choice I make;
2. Choices will be deemed as made whether they are made consciously, or unconsciously; and
3. The flow of life will be determined by what those choices are aligned to.

When I realised that everything else in the game is completely up to me, it gave me license to start looking at how I had set up my game so far, in order to begin developing some strategic changes and to create new directives to change the course of my life moving forwards.

I also realised that the trophy in the game of life isn't success and it's certainly not ticking all the boxes before you die. The trophy is happiness and you don't have to get to the end of your life before you're allowed to have it. It also doesn't have to be hard to get, or to keep.

Understanding this made it really easy for me to understand how simply I could engage with the three fixed rules of life.

If it was my choices that dictated how my life was going to respond, then I was going to start being very conscious and very specific in the choices I was making.

With the three fixed rules for life now firmly in my vision, I began to understand the importance of finding the threads that were attached to beliefs that had been holding me back. I started wandering along thought processes and uncovering things that had led me to repeating patterns. I then began to unwind them and recreate them in positive and empowering ways.

It is at about this stage that the power of overwhelm usually rears its head and steps in to create an obstacle to forward momentum. The most powerful weapon you have available to you in conquering overwhelm is to make sure that what you are doing is aligned with your values. When you understand the things that are most important to you, it's so much easier to take empowered, simple and manageable steps forwards. Your values will guide you and allow you to meet the overwhelm head on, and then move past it.

It is also critical to understand that you set up material constructs in your life as evidence that you are successful. For most of us, the way we judge where we are at is by being able to compare what we have against the things that others have. I can tell you this: there is not one material item that can assist you when you are on the floor, broken and unable to get back up again.

It was only the simplest, most basic aspects of life that I was able to abide when I was staring face first into the abyss. I turned to basic food, outdoor exercise and the company of my cat when I collapsed, and I could have very little of anything else in my space without becoming panicked and completely overwhelmed.

A question I am often asked when being interviewed is: *'How do you deal with the fear of changing your life and walking away from the things and the money that you had?'* This question is always positioned in the context of *'Let's face it, everyone would like to live differently but they have commitments, families and retirements to think about'*.

You can only live differently when you understand that your attachment to the material aspects of life is merely an excuse you've put in place, just so that you have something to hide behind. This might sound confronting, but everything I have seen tells me this is true.

If you want your life to be different, then it might be helpful to do at least one small thing differently today. However, doing one small thing differently today does not mean that you have to give up everything you are doing now. It simply means finding one step that can take you closer to the way you would like your life to be.

I discovered that the only way to give overwhelm the boot from my life was to refuse to engage in the thinking that it brings. Overwhelm is all about things being too big, too hard and too unachievable. The best way I have found to combat this thinking is to make your life all about simple steps that are really easy and completely achievable.

If you want to change your thinking, my suggestion would be to try to change the way you ask questions. Instead of coming up with all the reasons why you can't have something, consider asking questions about how you can do things differently. For example: *'What can I do in this situation so that I can feel better?'*

When 'how?' is the basic grounding of your life platform, the people, opinions, and obstacles fade away and you will be making conscious choices that drive your life in a different direction. Choose to find the pathway to *how* you can do things and give yourself every chance of dimming the power of those excuses that block you from engaging with your happiness.

NUFFdoms

Sometimes the easiest way to find direction in your life is to turn to the things that mean the most to you. We often find ourselves lost because we have spent too much time doing the things that other people have told us are right for us. When we spend our time immersed in the things that mean the most to us we can suddenly find our lives in a beautiful flow. Here's a few questions to help you find your way back to the things that mean the most to you:

1. Take a few moments to think about the things (people, places, experiences, activities and objects) that mean the most to you. Write them in the space below as they come to mind:

   _____
   _____
   _____
   _____
   _____
   _____
   _____

2. What are the things that drive you – the things you walk away from feeling great and full of energy? Write them in the space below:

   _____
   _____
   _____
   _____
   _____
   _____
   _____

3. Looking at your answers to questions 1 & 2, how many of them do you regularly have in your life right now? (Keep your answer to this simple – there's no need to justify or defend the answer – simply write it down and let it stand).

_____
_____
_____
_____
_____

4. Of the answers that you listed in questions 1 & 2 which one of them would you like to get more of in your life now?

_____
_____
_____
_____
_____

5. Why do you want more of it in your life? (Why is it important to you that you have more of it in your life now?)

_____
_____
_____
_____
_____
_____
_____

6. What are three steps you could take to bring that thing into your life now?

1. _____

2. _____

3. _____

4. Write down when, and how, you will take the first step listed in question 6:

_____
_____
_____
_____
_____
_____
_____
_____
_____
_____
_____
_____
_____

THE ECONOMY OF ENOUGH - *UNLOCKING THE SECRET TO HAPPILY EVER AFTER*

Notes

CHAPTER 7

"One of the drawbacks about adventures is that when you come to the most beautiful places you are often too anxious and hurried to appreciate them; so that Arvis (though she remembered them years later) had only a vague impression of grey lawns, quietly bubbling fountains, and the long black shadows of cypress trees."

– C.S. Lewis, *The Horse and His Boy*

Fear of Missing Out (FOMO)

There's nothing worse than that sense of rising panic that sits at the bottom of your throat and threatens to overwhelm you on a minute-by-minute basis. It comes with a foreboding sense of resignation that you'll never get 'it' right, and that you will never be able to shake it. Perhaps the worst thing about this panic is that it has now been with you for so long that you no longer remember what life is like without it; it's become the new baseline for your every day.

You try to stay upbeat and put a positive spin on everything because, well that's what you've been told will be your salvation. If you're not positive, then you won't be able to manifest effectively. You work hard on your manifestations, trying not to be despondent on the inside when they don't present in your life. All the while, you're smiling on the outside and desperately hoping that one day you'll get to be the one that finds that one little piece of information that means you can leap out of your life and suddenly live in the sun, with everything peachy and rosy all the time.

I used to think I was the only one that hid these thoughts inside – pushed down into the deep, dark recesses where no one could see them.

Then my first book *"Keep It Super Simple – Tips from a Recovering Perfectionist"* made its way into the world and I found myself talking to people from all around the globe and hearing that their stories held this common theme.

In fact, the more I talk to people, the more I understand why whole industries suddenly pop up and become multi-million-dollar scenarios, bringing with them buzz words and acronyms that we're all suddenly aware of. Then, we all start to sing and dance to the tune of these new industries because they tell us what we need to do to become more successful.

Seemingly overnight we saw the rise of the mindfulness and resilience industries. The first, mindfulness, to get us all to build ways for us to spend more time in the present moment. The second, resilience, for us to build some strength and determination, so that we aren't so knocked around by the world.

Unfortunately, these two things are the perfect example of why we should listen less to what we're being told we *have* to do and concentrate more on finding out the things that will work specifically for us as individuals.

I'm often engaged to deliver keynote speeches and workshops on mindfulness, and I believe that I'm asked to do so because I have a very different take on what mindfulness is, and how all of us can easily incorporate it into our lives.

When I present on mindfulness, I usually ask the attendees to raise their hands if they saw 'mindfulness' on the agenda and thought that I would be asking them to make their mind go blank for ten minutes. Almost always, 80% or more of the audience raise their hands.

The next thing I ask them is to be honest and leave their hand raised if they rolled their eyes and thought 'not this again'. Almost all of them keep their hands raised. You see, my experience with mindfulness is that it has been misconstrued as a limited field where, if you can't make your mind go blank for ten minutes, then you aren't mindful enough.

The mindfulness message has been dumbed down so much now that people think it relates to this one thing alone. And the reality of it is this: almost everyone finds it impossible to sit still and make their mind go blank for ten minutes. Mindfulness, therefore, has moved to being yet another thing that people are failing at – another sign that life is out of kilter and there is no way to get it back under control.

Here's the thing: we live in an over-stimulated, highly connected and extremely invasive lifetime where we are connected 24/7, we have information constantly coming at us in significant quantities, and our home, work and social lives are obsessively overlapping. There seems to be no escape, and every day seems to move faster and be more demanding. Our minds are going at a hundred miles an hour and we try harder and harder to fit more and more in.

We are expected to remember more, to do more and to be more, all at the same time as making ourselves a better person; after all, we've been told for decades all of the things that are wrong with us. We force ourselves to go to every event on offer – we have to, because otherwise we might miss our 'download', or that one 'golden nugget' of information we need. Our minds are stuck on what happens if we miss out and so the fear of missing out (FOMO) starts to drive our lives.

It's worth noting that, in the limited time that people get to spend in a workshop, it would be very difficult for them to learn to make their mind go blank; especially if it is a short workshop for only a couple of hours and then it's straight back to the work desk to get on with the day. The environment isn't conducive to assisting someone in quieting the mind. This type of training also doesn't take into account that everyone is an individual and therefore needs to find their own pathway to mindfulness.

Mindfulness is actually a fabulous thing that is highly effective when it can be brought into everyday life. Mindfulness is *absolutely* not about making your mind go blank for ten minutes. It's all about finding the process that allows you to connect consciously with the present moment, so that you can actually live your life and make conscious decisions that drive you forward in a connected way.

Because so many of us believe that being mindful is something that we just can't achieve, we revert back to our unconscious behaviour of reacting on auto-pilot. Before we know it, we're back into the busy game, running around and spreading ourselves thinly, and trying to make sure we don't miss anything, no matter how seemingly insignificant it might be in our lives.

The sad thing about this is that it now has such a significant hold on our lives that it has its own acronym – FOMO is everywhere. We try to lighten the significance by making a bit of a joke about it and accusing our friends laughingly that they're 'FOMOing' on, but the reality is that it does exist, and it is feeding the panic that sits just below the surface.

FOMO itself is a massive blocker to being mindful, because it feeds a deeply held fear that we've not achieved enough in life and that we have to drive ourselves harder before we can be successful. FOMO is a major contributor to the thought process that we must be stressed and exhausted before we're allowed to be successful, because without FOMO we wouldn't be driven to attend every event under the sun, so we don't miss out.

Then we see the rise of YOLO – 'You Only Live Once'. YOLO has come into existence because FOMO needs something to soften it. YOLO is the lever that is used to try and convince you that you must go to that event you were wavering over. If FOMO doesn't get you there, then YOLO is certain to. Either way, you won't be missing an event anytime soon if either of these two phenomena have a hold on you.

I realise now that not being good enough was more than just a thorn that was forever in my side; it was also the poison that ran through my veins, constantly feeding my stress, exhaustion and overwhelm. While these three things ran unchecked in my life, it also meant that I was always rooted to the spot and the panic that threatened to overtake me was never far from the surface.

One of the greatest gifts I now appreciate every day, having gone through my intensive and lengthy recovery process, is the amount of clarity I now have around the things that drove my life in unsupportive ways. From being stuck in my life and unable to see the way off the spiral of aching body, tired mind and weary bones, to being able to clearly see the construct that I had created to keep me frozen in place – these learnings were a revelation.

It seems to have happened all at once; one minute I was stuck and the next I was moving in a different direction. But I believe this was because I was also stuck in a mindset of being unable to acknowledge any advancement or goodness in myself or the work I was doing in the world.

Deep down in my soul, I believed I was a good person, but I had endured so many decades of messaging that told me I was bad or evil that I struggled to be able to admit that what I was doing was good enough, and that I was a worthy participant in society.

As I started to take steps in my life in a different way, by giving them a different emphasis and infusing them with love and adventure, I was able to also take the time to acknowledge the power of every step.

When you give each step the credit it is due then it's easy to see how they all go together to create an end result that is far from the place from which you started out.

I also found that as each step became more consciously directed, my steps were made more in alignment with who I am. That also meant that it took less effort to actually make a step happen. With less effort required, it created space for me to understand that my mind had been sending me very specific directions for decades and I had been misunderstanding what it had been saying. I used to be frozen in place whenever I experienced the sensation of being terrified about something. Terror was always a catalyst for perfection to raise its head.

As stress and exhaustion lost their hold in my life, and I began to live in a way that was easier and more in flow, I realised that when I felt terrified it was actually a signal showing me where my next step lay. I had needed to create a signal at that level because I had switched off so many of my emotions, so much so that I couldn't feel anything anymore. By creating an emotion at the level of terror, my mind was hoping that I might finally take notice.

For me to overcome the impact of not being good enough, I had to learn to eliminate the impact that FOMO was having on my life. I had to understand the things that are important to me and make them my priorities. I also had to make sure that time was allocated every day to these priorities, and to learn to defend that time vigorously – allowing flexibility where it was needed but dedicating time to these things as a general rule.

Life is such a fabulous thing to live when you take your steps aligned with who you are. And, even better, it's really easy to live it differently when you take the time to understand what is important to you.

Sure, there are times when I find myself taking a deep breath before I can take the step in front of me; in fact, I find that that is happening more often now, not less. But taking that breath is not such a big thing anymore; I'm no longer frozen in place by the fear of what someone else might think about me, or whether or not someone approves of what I am doing.

I'm not worried about whether my choices to do or not to do something mean that I'm going to miss out. More often than not, the breath is giving me time to process the enormity of the step I am about to take and allowing me to savour the thrill of excitement that the little adrenalin rush gives me as I think about the possibilities that the step might bring.

NUFFdoms

When the world you live in is ruled by FOMO you spend your time chasing your tail and wasting your energy – progressively making yourself transparent until you can no longer see who you are anymore.

The first place to start to gain control back in your life, and to lessen the impact of FOMO, is to ask yourself the following questions that will allow you to be a little bit kinder to yourself:

1. Take a few moments to consider what you are filling your days with. We're all busy, but when do we actually stop to look at what we're busy doing:

   _____
   _____
   _____
   _____
   _____
   _____
   _____

2. For each thing you've listed above, write down WHY you are doing them:

   _____
   _____
   _____
   _____
   _____
   _____
   _____

3. A lot of the time we find ourselves doing things because we've said 'Yes' on auto-pilot. How many of the things you listed at question 1 are you doing because you didn't really thing about it before saying 'Yes'?

_____

_____

_____

_____

4. Write down the things you think you need for you to feel better right now? What do you need to have, or have happen, for you to feel okay and like you could stop having to chase every opportunity?

_____

_____

_____

_____

5. What are three simple steps you could take that would move you towards having the things (or even one of the things) you listed in question 4?

_____

_____

_____

_____

6. When and how will you take the first of these steps?

_____

_____

_____

Notes

CHAPTER 8

"I promise you nothing is as chaotic as it seems. Nothing is worth diminishing your health. Nothing is worth poisoning yourself into stress, anxiety, and fear."

– Steve Maraboli

Soldier On

There was a time when I used to believe that if it wasn't painful, then I didn't deserve to have it in my life. I wasn't conscious of this belief, but it ruled my life nonetheless.

I slogged my way through every day, deep within the haze and the fog of exhaustion. Every step was clouded by stress and low self-esteem. It was hard to keep going and, in general, a pretty miserable existence.

There's a beautiful saying that goes like this: *'you can't see the wood for the trees'* and looking back now, that's how I feel about where my life was at. I had set my life up to revolve around a complex set of rules, rules that were established to ensure that I could never achieve success. I spent every day worrying about what might happen next, fretting over who would say what, wondering how I could respond, agonising over what the impact would be and trying to work out whether I could get through it all without experiencing any more pain.

There was no corner of my life that wasn't set up this way. Even those places in my life that had finally created too big an impact – forcing me to walk away from them – constantly threatened to overrun me.

To survive in this environment, I had to shut myself down so that I could lessen the pain of living in this way. I became like a robot, working on auto-pilot and responding from an emotionless platform. Yes, there were times when I would feel the emotion of a situation, but then I would resolutely shove it down inside and quickly move on.

I had mastered the art of 'soldier on'.

Like so many others, I had seen the advertising campaigns that provide products that help us to do just that – soldier on – through those times in life when our bodies are telling us that we should be resting. I had grabbed those 'remedies' with both hands, believing that they would keep me going.

Whether it's a pharmaceutical drug that masks the symptoms of disease, or some form of strapping that masks the pain of inflammation, a drink that fuels your body with chemically-induced energy or any of the other artificial sources that give us a false sense of power, all of them can only sustain you for a limited period of time before you have to pay the price for using them.

We are divinely built beings, and the minute we step into a belief that we can turn to using these artificial things to prop us up, we effectively sign a contract with ourselves to ensure our own destruction.

We use that artificial energy source to allow us to push through, no matter the consequence. In fact, like many others, I was so engrossed in a life that over-delivered to everyone around me that I didn't even give the fact that there may be consequences for using those sources a second – let alone first – thought.

I was also totally oblivious to the knowledge that I was living with an extreme level of pain. Every step took an enormous amount of energy and willpower, and I had absolutely no idea that the very life within me was being dangerously drained away *every day*. My baseline experience of what it took to live my life had moved to such an extreme point that I could no longer feel the weight that I was carrying through every day.

I liken this pain to my experiences following on from serious knee surgery, where I elected to have the surgeries on both knees completed at the same time. I have always had a very high tolerance to pain, so whilst the recovery from surgery was painful, it was nothing that I couldn't bear. The problem with this was that I ended up settling on a new baseline for what was a 'normal' feeling in my knees.

Sure, they were better than they were before the surgery, with significantly less sharp and 'jagging' pain under my knee caps. I could actually go for a walk without too many problems, and they had far less stiffness after sitting still for a period of time. But they were still really painful when walking up and down stairs or traversing hills, and they were still very stiff upon waking. In short, the issues in my knees had not been completely resolved but because they were better than they were before, I settled for a life that had less pain than I previously felt.

Fast forward eighteen months, I found myself experiencing significant pain in my knees again and I could no longer convince myself that the pain baseline was normal. So, I returned to my surgeon, and he recommended that I have further surgery to remove the pins that had been screwed into my shins as part of the previous surgeries.

After the follow-up surgery to remove the pins, I was restricted from any form of exercise that involved my legs for at least ten days. But by day six I was going insane from sitting still, so I decided to go for a walk. The absolute revelation of walking with significantly reduced pain post-surgery is something I still struggle to explain. Until that moment, I had no idea of the level of pain that I had accepted as 'normal' in my life. It wasn't until that moment of clarity that I started to understand my ability to cloud my own vision and keep myself standing in place.

Those first steps after that surgery heralded the very beginnings of the rumblings and disquiet in my mind. It wouldn't be until a few years later that I would find myself in a position where I was forced to delve more deeply into how my mind worked, but those steps unlocked the door, ready for me to open it and walk through.

And when I did open that door, my vista expanded into a world of discovery, exploration and adventure. Because I collapsed and my whole world shattered around me, everything in my life demanded attention, all at once. Every inch of my life was suddenly clamouring for attention, and the noise of that clamouring was almost unbearable.

I had to find a way to quieten the noise; otherwise, I was going to go mad. So, I taught myself to create virtual shelves in my mind. I pictured a room that looked a bit like a walk-in wardrobe that had lots of shelves and drawers, and in those shelves and drawers I created storage boxes. Into each of the boxes, I placed all the different things that were demanding my attention. As I placed each thing into its own box and allocated it a place on a shelf or in a drawer, I reminded myself that I knew where everything was and that I could come back to each item, one at a time, when I was ready to do so.

Doing this allowed me to separate all of the different things that were trying to get my attention but it also allowed me a bit of time and space to simply breathe.

Before my breakdown, I was a highly organised and disciplined person – everything was systemised, followed a process and operated on a tight schedule. When I collapsed, the impact was so intense that I was unable to think clearly or process anything cognitively, and it seemed as though any ability to be disciplined was lost to me.

For the first time in my life, I was unable to muster the strength to *soldier on* – there was literally no energy left in the tank to create the strength needed to keep going, so it simply wasn't an option for me any longer.

I had to find another way to move forward, and since punishment and pain had been the order of the day for me previously, I swung to the other end of the pendulum and started to explore love, ease and grace as the primary filters I would apply to my life.

When I viewed the world through these lenses, it allowed me to pick up each thing that demanded my attention one at a time. As I looked at each thing, I started by separating the emotion from the information.

It might sound weird, but I did this by holding out both my hands, visualising the thing that was demanding my attention and asking it to place the emotion in my left hand and the information in my right hand.

Then I asked the emotion sitting in my left hand to sit quietly and allow me the space to look more closely at the 'stuff' sitting in my right hand.

As I looked more closely at the information in my right hand, I found myself asking some questions; for example:

'What is the benefit of this information?'

'Has having this thing in my life benefited me?'

'What have I achieved by pushing through and making these things happen?'

'What reasons have I had for allowing this thing to be in my life?'

And as I asked these questions, I began to find clarity around what life was like when you allow yourself to rest when you need to and move forward when you're refreshed.

Trust me, I know how weird this sounds. But before your mind sets in and you start to get all wrapped up in whether or not this is all a bit too 'woo-woo', allow yourself to suspend all your conditioning to date and see that it was a process that worked for me.

Yes, it was outside the box and totally different from the way I had done things before. But that's probably why it worked so beautifully for me; it was non-threatening, and my mind didn't really have any judgement parameters in place to try and stop it from assisting me.

Surprisingly, it was also a really easy process to follow. It was the first time in my life that I realised that life didn't always have to be challenging. I experienced for myself how easy it can be to move your life in a different way, without it being so painful that you cringe and turn away before you even start the process. And because I based the process I used on ease and grace, it also allowed me to find the answers to my questions without feeling the full onslaught of having failed because I got it wrong along the way.

I learned two very valuable lessons through bringing this process into my life: you don't have to change everything at once, and it's okay to rest when you are tired.

As I moved through the process of looking at each piece of myself in turn, there were some things that were simply too big for me to look at, given the state of mind that I was in. Instead of allowing this to stop me and revert me back onto the path I had left, I simply put that piece back into its box with an acknowledgment of its existence and a promise that I would return to look at it when I could.

This was a really important step to take. It meant that I wasn't making excuses as to why that thing was in my life, why I had to keep doing things in a certain way, or why I couldn't do anything about it. Rather, I was simply acknowledging that it was there and promising that I would come back and look at it again.

This dropped the pressure and the stress attached to the item, but it also cut any opportunity that may have arisen for me to step back into a negative emotional connection to the item. Bluntly, this situation would have been a perfect breeding ground for 'not enough' to arise, and it was critical that I ensured that a filter of love was applied so that I could come back to it when I was ready.

This transformation has been *literally* life-changing. Previously, I lived a life of pushing through and *soldiering on* for decades and wound up on the floor, unable to get back up.

I am living proof that masking the signals we receive from our body, telling us that we've pushed ourselves too far, doesn't work. We don't have to kick a winning goal in every second of every minute in our lives.

It is okay for us to rest when we need it.

I can tell you from personal experience that when you break yourself completely, there will be nothing left for you to give to anyone else. And, while you're enmeshed in recovering, the world will move on and turn around you.

Rest, refuel and give up the soldiering. You'll be surprised at just how much further you can go!

NUFFdoms

If we continuously push through the warning signs in our life then we drive ourselves to significant ill health and strain our ability to thrive in our life. We also create constructs and paradigms in our life that are less than optimal and we end up living our lives in a dull and drained way.

To help you better identify the signals that your body and mind are giving you that you might need to take some time to rest and/or redefine some areas of your life, these questions often help to get you thinking in a slightly different way:

1. Write down the areas in your life that you're constantly pushing yourself (think things like when you're sick you either go to work anyway or you 'work from home', you're constantly taking or drinking supplements to give you energy, you constantly take work home, you always say 'Yes' when people ask you to do things and the list goes on!!):

   _____

   _____

   _____

   _____

   _____

   _____

2. Ask yourself the question: *'Is living like this working for me?'* (this is a 'Yes' or 'No' answer – resist the temptation to justify or defend the answer; simply let the answer stand on its own):

   _____

   _____

   _____

3. Write down what you think you have achieved by pushing through the things you listed in question 1:

_____
_____
_____
_____
_____
_____

4. What are your reasons for having allowed the things listed at question 1 to remain in your life:

_____
_____
_____
_____
_____

5. Given the way you feel now – your energy levels, level of exhaustion and health (physical and mental) in general, would you say that it is wise for you to continue having the things listed at question 1 remain in your life moving forwards (this is a 'Yes' or 'No' answer)?

_____
_____
_____
_____
_____

6. Looking at the list of things in question 1, which thing do you think you could easily do differently now?

_____
_____
_____
_____
_____

7. What are three steps you can take to do the thing you identified in question 6 differently now?

   1. _____

   2. _____

   3. _____

8. Write down when and how you will take step 1 listed above:

_____
_____
_____
_____
_____
_____

Notes

CHAPTER 9

"But if thought corrupts language, language can also corrupt thought."

– *George Orwell, 1984*

Live and Let Live

There's a glaring dichotomy in the way we're taught to live our lives. On the one hand, we're socially conditioned when we're young to ensure that we behave and live in an acceptable manner. On the other, as we grow older and we come up against tougher times, we're told that we should 'just be ourselves' and that it doesn't matter what others think about us.

These two ways of thinking are poles apart from each other. The first is embedded within us through the conditioning process when we are young. This process teaches us the things about ourselves that others perceive to be good or bad, right or wrong, and so on. It is in our formative years that we're taught the pain and ostracism of having a part of ourselves that others think is wrong and the pleasure of love and acceptance for the things that others decide are our 'good' characteristics.

Initially, our social conditioning starts within the family environment. Then, as we grow and develop, and our circle of influence starts to widen, we begin to assimilate further into the community. For most of us, our circle starts to widen when we first attend school, and it

is here that we come face to face with the opinions, perceptions and conditioning of people outside our family environment. Suddenly, some of the things that we've been taught are good traits to have are perceived by others as bad ones. Before we know it, we're hurt and confused by the feedback and mixed messages we're being given, and we start to construct a whole new list of good and bad things about ourselves.

What happens when you're young and the things you've been taught to believe are good about yourself are the things that others have suddenly decided are 'bad'? You feel the pain to the very core of your being when you see the scorn in another person's eyes and know that while you can't understand why, it is directed at you. Your world is rocked, the hurt grabs you in the heart and you go home lost, injured and feeling very alone.

It is usually at this point that the second way of thinking is introduced, and you receive the conflicting instruction that *'it doesn't matter what other people think of you'* and that *'it is OK to be yourself'*.

Now it's really confusing to work out what is right and wrong anymore! The goalposts seem to be forever changing and you simply cannot please anyone. Survival instincts then kick in and you learn to be a chameleon that can morph and change depending on the situation you find yourself in. You eventually work out how you can be one shape at school and another at home – and sometimes even another shape again when you're with your friends. Potentially, the more you expand your activities the more versions of yourself you might need to create.

You don't realise it at the time, but this process of creating multiple versions of yourself is exhausting! The conflict that this creates within ourselves is significant; it impacts our confidence, engenders low self-esteem and almost certainly ensures that we are unable to make decisions for ourselves and our lives.

As someone who struggled with perfectionism, mastering the ability to morph as a chameleon was my primary camouflage. Slotting in under the radar was the perfect solution for me in almost every situation. I had no desire to stand out, be noticed or be the object of attention, and I mastered the art of hiding in plain sight. That is, except for when I was playing sports or in situations where I found myself with an almost uncontrollable need to protect people who were being bullied or picked on by others.

Despite having mastered the ability to hide my emotion behind a perfect façade, inside I was actually very sensitive, and it hurt me a lot if I became the subject of someone's ridicule. After all, if someone else had something mean or hurtful to say about me, this was simply an abject reminder to me that I was being publicly exposed as failing in my drive to perfection.

I am relatively tall – I was always in the back row in all the school photos – and from a very early age I was always a lot taller than most of the other girls my age. My innate desire to fade into the background was completely at odds with being so much taller than almost everyone around me. I was extremely conscious of how much I stood out. However, there were two instances where I allowed my height to serve a useful purpose.

The first of these was when I was playing sport. I had long arms, long legs and the gift of excellent coordination, so I could easily use my height to my best advantage.

The second instance, where I used my height to excellent effect, was when going into battle for others. I was driven to protect those whom I perceived could not protect themselves. If someone was being picked on for their hair, their clothes, their scholastic ability… and the list goes on, then I was unable to help myself; I had to step in. Not only was I tall, but I also had the ability to muster a really imposing demeanour and my version of standing up for someone was to engage in a verbal contest with their persecutor. Of course, this almost always turned the heat directly onto me, but for some reason it didn't seem to hurt as much because I'd been of 'service' to someone else in the process.

It wasn't until I had to look at these aspects of my life – when all the pieces of myself had shattered on the floor during the throes of my breakdown – that I took the time to really understand how these threads wove together to create limiting patterns in my life.

Shining the light on these pieces and allowing myself the time and space to look at them without any emotion, meant that I could better understand the role I had given them and the havoc I had allowed them to wreak. When I stopped to think about the actual impact of the dichotomy of my conditioning – 'right or wrong, good or bad' versus 'it's OK to be yourself' – I was suddenly exposed to feeling the full force of the emptiness that had formed within myself. There was a gaping hole full of other people's 'stuff' that had formed to keep the two sides of that conditioning separate, and I had to learn how to close the gap, allow myself to heal and become whole again.

A significant part of this was excising all of that 'stuff' that wasn't mine.

By far the greatest understanding I learned whilst shining the light on these pieces was that from a very young age we are trained to be judgemental. We are taught to determine our progress by comparing ourselves to others around us, judging where they are at and then holding that judgement as a yardstick against our own progress.

We use the reactions, actions and behaviours of others around us to gauge whether we're acceptable, and to obtain direct feedback on what we need to change, remove and hide of ourselves. We also undertake different activities, take on different jobs, live in certain places, drive certain cars, adopt particular hobbies and sometimes associate with certain people who aren't aligned with who we truly are. We do this so that we can influence the opinion, and therefore the feedback, we receive on how we're living up to other people's standards. We live under the weight of that judgement, and we find ourselves constantly morphing and reshaping ourselves to 'fit in' with the world around us – *to fit in with who the outside world says we should be.*

Judgement is such an innate tool used by all of us that we apply without thought. It has become an auto-pilot reaction that allows us to quickly determine whether what we are seeing around us is something that can take us forward, threaten our position in society, keep the status quo or challenge the way of life as we know it.

We ebb and flow through life using our power to force change on others. Or, we shrink into submission under the force of someone else's demands, depending on the environment and the company we keep. We bend to the threat of ostracism and create the version of ourselves that we think is the most acceptable for the situation we find ourselves in.

We pack our lives full of meaningless, material 'stuff' so that we can further influence the perception of others around us. We build a façade of ourselves that gives others a glimpse, or an impression, of who we are. Little do we realise that what we are actually building is a construct that confines us and serves only to distract us and limit our ability to fully step into our greatness.

What if I told you that, as part of learning about the impact of allowing myself to be a chameleon, I also gained bucket loads of clarity about the role that judgement plays, and why we are so willing to allow it to run free in our lives?

I see this so often in the people I work with and, particularly, in the people who are in an audience when I speak. Here are two of the most common things that people say to me after they hear me talk: *'you're amazing, there is no way I could ever achieve anything like what you have achieved'*, and *'my life is nowhere near as overwhelming as yours'*.

Having recovered from the depths of a very deep, dark, black hole, and having come out the other side with so much more understanding of life, I am constantly floored that as human beings we have allowed ourselves to be squashed and remain that way for so long. Now, when I'm talking to people after they've heard my keynote speech, I always have this to offer:

> *Instead of comparing yourself to others, and judging yourself as lacking, find the things that you have in common and start there.*

We all have our own stories – we're all here to live our own lives and master our own destinies. We might have some things that are similar in our lives, but if we all do exactly the same thing then we're all holding ourselves back.

It was a very confronting moment when I realised that judgement, and the way that I had let it completely rule my life, was nothing more than a *distraction* that I was constantly using to avoid learning what I needed to learn so that I could be the biggest possible version of myself.

The weight of this understanding was initially staggering and, at first, I didn't want to believe that what I had uncovered was true. But the longer I looked at it, the clearer it all became.

Every second I spent critiquing someone else's life choices, behaviour, personality and so on was a second that I was wasting on following through with my own development. Suddenly, instead of being triggered by someone's behaviour and reacting on auto-pilot to try and 'pull them into line' – or berating myself for not being good enough in comparison – I became aware that there was a deeper meaning to what I was being shown. I understood that the behaviour was a message for me to stop and consider what it was about the behaviour that had upset me so much.

In short, I learned to separate the person from the behaviour. Instead of allowing my emotion to run my life, I started asking myself questions so that I could learn what I needed to learn *from myself*.

I started to understand that whilst the decision another unique individual made to behave in a particular way might not be 'acceptable' to me, it may well have been perfectly fine from their own perspective. Importantly, I understood that even though there might have been a divide in the 'acceptance' of that behaviour, the other person's decision could only affect me if I chose to let it.

I started to play with creating a construct that would allow me to drop judgement from my repertoire and acknowledge behaviour as being aligned with who I was, or not. I found myself adopting a 'live and let live' mindset, where everyone is respected for their individualism and their uniqueness. This is a world where I can choose the behaviour and characteristics that I am aligned with *and so can everyone else*.

My life choices don't always match those of others and nor should they, because I choose them based on what is right for me.

If I experience a situation where there is behaviour around me that doesn't sit well, then I simply identify the behaviour as something that I don't choose to have in my life. I then honour the person for the unique human being that they are and the choices that they can make *for their own life*.

When I created a life that allowed me to drop the judgement, I was also able to drop the influence that any superiority or inferiority complexes had in my life. There was no longer a battle to be had with being good enough because life was no longer about 'enough'. Life had become about being aligned or not.

By choosing to move to a life that was ruled by the 'live and let live' principle, I also had to accept that what other people think of me is none of my business. Other people's opinions and perceptions of you, your behaviour, your choices and your actions are always coloured by the filters they use and the limited information they are working from. In understanding this, I became free to turn my focus onto *my* life and the choices I was making within it.

When you've been taught that change is hard – as most of us have – it can be tricky to try something different when you first start. It was the same for me; I had hooked into the 'change is hard' belief just like everyone else. However, I was able to acknowledge that the way I had been living my life wasn't working for me, so I made the decision to try something new.

After some trial and error and playing around with a few different ways of doing things, I eventually found the easiest way for me to drop judgement and make my own decisions was to allow myself the freedom to retrain my thought processes with love, ease and grace.

NUFFdoms

The more we allow judgement to run our life, the more we will be pulled away from the path that leads us to the simplest and easiest version of our lives. If you want to learn to take back control of your thoughts, actions and reactions then try asking yourself these practical questions when you're faced with something that starts to get your blood boiling!

1. Think about a time when you saw someone exhibiting a behaviour that made your thoughts turn to disapproval. Write down what this behaviour was:

   _____
   _____
   _____
   _____
   _____
   _____
   _____

2. When you think about the behaviour that you saw, what was your reaction (don't worry about whether or not the reaction was good, bad, warranted or not – simply allow the words to be written down and let them stand without any judgement):

   _____
   _____
   _____
   _____
   _____
   _____
   _____

3. Take a moment to write down how it made you feel when you reacted in the way you wrote down in question 2:

_____
_____
_____
_____
_____
_____

4. Did the feelings you wrote about in question 3 give you energy or take energy away from you?

_____
_____
_____
_____
_____

5. Visualise the behaviour happening in that situation again. This time, instead of reacting automatically, change the scene in your head and see yourself asking the question: *'Is this behaviour aligned with my values?'* Write your answer to this question down:

_____
_____
_____
_____
_____
_____

6. If your answer to question 5 was 'No', see yourself making the following statement to yourself:

    'That behaviour doesn't align with my values therefore I am consciously choosing not to connect with its energy. I choose to move forward aligned to <insert whatever behaviour is aligned with your values>'.

    Write down how using this statement made you feel:

    _____
    _____
    _____
    _____
    _____
    _____
    _____
    _____

7. If your answer to question 5 was 'Yes', write down why the behaviour you witnessed upset you so much:

    _____
    _____
    _____
    _____
    _____
    _____
    _____
    _____

Notes

CHAPTER 10

"Passion is energy. Feel the power that comes from focusing on what excites you."

– Oprah Winfrey

Energy Rules

My world, now, is very different than before and I share my journey with the world in a way that challenges the status quo.

As a result, I find myself being interviewed or asked to speak in all sorts of places, all around the world. Whilst every place is unique with its own culture and its own sense of community, there are a few common threads that appear almost everywhere.

One of those threads is the sheer exhaustion that people are facing as an everyday norm. It's something that I experienced myself, and it wasn't until I dropped and couldn't get back up again that I started to learn about the consequences of pushing too hard, for too long. Perhaps most importantly, I've realised that there is nothing normal about having chronic levels of stress and exhaustion in your life.

Somehow, we've allowed ourselves to believe that being constantly stressed and exhausted is the only way that we can be successful – in fact, most of us believe that it is impossible to be successful without it. I had even convinced myself that I *thrived* on stress, that when I was stressed was when I would produce my best work.

As I learned about the effects of stress and exhaustion on the body and the mind, I began to understand how easy it was to be stuck in a cycle that repeated itself relentlessly. The tougher and stronger I was, the easier it was for me to be sucked into the cycle and for it to consume me.

When I first experienced my breakdown, it was like being hit by a tidal wave of emotion. It was all consuming and completely overwhelming. It dulled all my senses and, even though I live in a first world environment, I went straight into survival mode. This moment signalled the beginning of a rollercoaster ride of epic proportions that would see me struggle to balance my energy for a significant period of time.

I had days when I would feel alright upon waking but being completely exhausted within two hours. Other days, I would wake feeling like I had been run over by a massive truck.

> *Often, I wondered whether I had damaged my system so significantly that I would never recover.*

I had no idea just how badly I had depleted my energy resources. It took me over four years to rebuild them to a stage where my energy levels were evened out again, and I had the fuel I needed to be able to easily do the things I wanted to do.

Most of us believe that our energy comes from the things that we eat. Whilst it is important to nourish the body by eating food that works for us, our energy is regenerated in a number of different ways.

We need energy to support us in all aspects of our life. We need it to fuel our drive and our passion for the things that are important to us. Without a well-fuelled energy tank, it's very hard to maintain forward momentum, and when our momentum is under strain we're less likely to achieve our goals in life.

Without energy, our lives become grey and colourless, with every activity feeling like it's a slog. Of course, as soon as we're in this environment we automatically drain more energy from our tank because our life is out of flow. We're straining to make things happen, we're relying on our inner strength to get us through and we're slowly draining the life out of ourselves, which ultimately means that our life becomes merely an existence.

Whenever I'm engaged to speak on the topics of work/life balance, resilience or energy management, I almost always talk to the audience about what my typical day used to look like:

> My alarm used to go off in the morning and my first thought for the day was: *'It can't possibly be time to get up yet!'* This thought would then be followed by: *'I'll get to the shower – surely that will make me feel better'*. Then my mind would turn to getting my aching, stiff and sore body moving, so that I could slowly and painfully drag myself out of bed. Once in the shower I would apply my will to making my body move, saying to myself: *'Just get moving – then you can get into the day'*.
>
> When the shower didn't help me, I would start the rushed process to get dressed, shovel some food down quickly and bolt out the door to get to the office as early as possible – almost as if the rush would magically generate the energy I needed to get going. At the office, I would deal with everyone else's needs, crises and emergencies.
>
> Then, almost as an encore performance, I'd come home, smash myself at the gym, organise dinner and then open up the laptop to get *my own* work for the day done.
>
> I'd head to bed exhausted, only for my mind to kick in and start going over what had happened during the day and stress about what might happen tomorrow. Eventually, I would fall into a disturbed, interrupted sleep which would last for about two hours before the alarm went off and the whole cycle started again.

Once I've finished explaining what my typical day used to look like, I always ask the audience this simple question: *'How many of you have days that look like this?'*

Without fail, at least 80% of every audience puts their hand up and I'd say that there are probably a few more in the audience who are too shy to let others know they also struggle in this area.

I used to think that I was on my own with the exhaustion struggle. I absolutely absorbed the lesson of 'be grateful for your lot in life because someone else has it a lot tougher than you' and I learned from a very early age to 'soldier on'.

In the process of rebuilding version 2.0 of myself, I found that I needed to acknowledge the depth of my inner strength. That strength has seen me through some really tough times and has been my absolute saviour on too many occasions to count. In acknowledging this, I also had to accept that my inner strength is not only my greatest strength – it is also my greatest weakness. My ability to turn on the energy booster jets with a simple thought is incredible; it's such an amazing ability to have. It's also an incredibly dangerous weapon to have in the tool kit, especially when it is used without any thought for the impact on my physical and mental systems if it isn't followed up with regenerating activities.

> *Just like military fast jets which have afterburners,*
> *it works a treat, until you run out of fuel.*

Like most people, I had no knowledge of the importance of our energy tanks and why we need them to be constantly refuelled for us to move forwards every day. I had blindly mastered an ability to propel myself forward with no knowledge about what that ability was actually doing to me. I focused wholly on delivering outcomes to everyone around me, making sure that they were okay and that all their needs were met, and I was completely oblivious to the fact that I was slowly killing myself while I was doing it.

The more I learned, the more I realised how little I knew about energy and how it is generated in our bodies and, more worryingly, how little I understood about the effects on both physical and mental health that come from keeping the body under constant strain, stress and exhaustion.

For example, I had no idea that allowing myself to be under constant stress meant that my entire nervous system was constantly in 'fight or flight' mode. This meant that almost all of my organs were constantly in hiatus and therefore not able to do the jobs they were supposed to be doing. It's little wonder that my whole digestive system was toxic, and I was struggling with something as simple as digesting the food I was eating. By allowing myself to be stressed, I was sending a command signal to my body that was blocking my ability to extract the vitamins and minerals from the food I was eating. So, although I was eating regularly and well, my body behaved as if it was malnourished and starving.

I also didn't know that by putting myself under constant stress and constantly demanding that my body stay in fight or flight mode, that I was also creating a cycle that made it next to impossible for me to sleep. Fight or flight mode puts your body on high alert and sends adrenalin and cortisol flooding through your system. It uses a massive amount of energy and saturates your body with those hormones so that you can run or fight for your survival as needed. It's very difficult to relax and allow your body to sleep when you have this chemical reaction happening inside.

The more I didn't sleep, the more exhausted I became and this led inevitably to even more increased stress. As a result, my body remained in fight or flight mode for longer and that in turn meant I couldn't sleep. And the cycle continued without end.

I continued to hammer on through this cycle for over twelve years. In the end, it was sheer strength of mind alone that kept me upright, but that too gave way and left me with only one option: a total and utter crash and burn.

As with all challenging experiences in life, my journey gave me the opportunity to learn and master new information. As I struggled with lagging energy – where some days all I could do was drag myself to the couch and stare mindlessly at the television screen – I started to learn about where our energy comes from and the ways in which it is attuned to us individually.

There was a great deal of information that presented itself to me so that I could learn, absorb and grow. The information which gave me the clearest picture about our energy, and how we can easily regenerate it, came in the form of the introvert/extrovert spectrum.

Most people believe that an introvert is someone who is shy and an extrovert is someone who is outgoing. However, the introvert/extrovert spectrum is actually all about the ways in which we re-energise ourselves.

It's much more detailed than this but suffice to say an extrovert is usually someone who is energised by, and thrives on, being around other people. They are rejuvenated by activities that are high energy, have lots of noise and lots of people – think loud bars, concerts, busy workplaces, crowded places and fitness classes such as Zumba and Boot Camp.

Introverts, on the other hand, are people whose energy tends to expand through reflection. An introvert is likely to re-energise through solitary activities such as hiking, reading, writing, meditating and through the application of mind/body disciplines such as yoga, tai chi and qi gong.

In recent years, the spectrum has been updated and it is now thought that there is likely a third category on the spectrum: 'Ambiversion'. This category captures those who fall towards the middle of the spectrum. An ambivert arguably has the best of both worlds, as they are likely to tap into the strengths of both the extroverts and the introverts. However, they do tend to fall into one category or the other for the way in which they ultimately re-energise themselves.

For example, an ambivert who has introvert tendencies will likely get a kick out of working with a team, but at some point, they will reach an invisible barrier that will tell them that they need to regroup and recharge on their own in a solitary activity. The same phenomenon occurs in reverse for an ambivert with extrovert tendencies.

When I first learned about the spectrum, it was one of those moments when the light goes on and you suddenly have so much clarity about the way things have gone so far, and how you can change them moving forwards. In the blink of an eye, I understood why I was so exhausted all the time. All of my research has shown me that that I am ambivert with introvert tendencies, but not knowing this meant that I was always living in the extroverted world. I was never doing any activities that were re-energising my batteries, which meant that I was always draining energy from an already empty tank.

With the benefit and wisdom of hindsight, I know that I kept very well hidden the fact that the way I was living wasn't good for me. I knew that I needed to do something differently, but I was afraid that it meant that I would have to change everything in my life, and I simply did not know where to start for me to do things differently.

> *I didn't realise that being exhausted didn't mean I had to quit everything I was doing – it simply meant that I needed to rest.*

One of the things I see a lot now when I am working with people in all corners of the world is this: people are frozen in place by the fear that they have to start everything in their lives again. We have been so successfully taught that change is hard and that it must be feared, that we would rather drive ourselves to an early death than take a single step in a slightly different way.

Understanding that you can live your life very differently, simply by understanding how your energy works, is the first step in creating a more fulfilling life for yourself. The second step is in understanding some of the simple questions you can ask yourself so that you can make a few decisions in a more conscious and gentle way.

NUFFdoms

Most of us have energy levels that are all over the place. There are moments when we feel like we have a surge of energy, but then suddenly we're exhausted and it feels like every step we take is a monumental struggle. Understanding how we refuel our energy tanks is critical to us ensuring that we're not just draining energy in the things we are doing. We need to refuel our energy source every day to make sure we have the energy we need to keep us moving forward in our lives.

1. Take a moment to write down the people, places and things that you always come away from feeling good. These are the things that you make you smile, laugh and generally feel good. You feel buoyant after doing them or spending time with or around them.

   _____
   _____
   _____
   _____
   _____

2. Take a moment to think about how your average day looks from an energy perspective. Write down how your energy levels flow throughout each day:

	Time of Day	Energy Level (High/Low)
1.		
2.		
3.		
4.		

3. Have a think about the activities you can be completing at different times. Write down the activities you feel you should be doing in the different times, making sure you include those activities that you have identified will make you feel great:

	Activities for different times of the day	
1.	Time: Activities: – – – –	Energy (high/low): – – – –
2.	Time: Activities: – – – –	Energy (high/low): – – – –
3.	Time: Activities: – – – –	Energy (high/low): – – – –
4.	Time: Activities: – – – –	Energy (high/low): – – – –

By allocating different activities to different times of the day you can better allocate high energy activities to high energy periods of time and lower energy activities to those times of the day that your energy naturally drops.

This also allows you more conscious connection time to make sure that you include activities that will re-energise you in those periods of time when your energy is lower.

For some of us, we don't always have complete control over what we do and when we get to do it, however there are always some things that we can control. Understanding where these things best fit into our day helps to assist us in ensuring that we are regularly doing things that support us in filling up our energy tanks rather than just draining from them constantly.

Notes

CHAPTER 11

> "We seldom realise, for example that our most private thoughts and emotions are not actually our own. For we think in terms of languages and images which we did not invent, but which were given to us by our society."
>
> – Alan W. Watts

Hidden Messages

We are all – each and every one of us – brainwashed in some way.

Whenever I talk about brainwashing, whether it be to a group or an individual, most people get very uncomfortable and immediately start to deny that this is true for them. We've been trained to believe that brainwashing is an indoctrination process that results in the impairment of our ability to think independently and form our own beliefs and affiliations.

'*That might be true for other people – but definitely isn't true for me because ...*' is often the response that I get when I start talking about all of us having been brainwashed. Most people think that brainwashing is something that only happens to those who get caught up in a cult, so it can't possibly be applicable to them.

Whilst we like to think that we are free-thinking, individual spirits, the reality is that we're all socially conditioned – that is, *brainwashed* – to some degree as we grow up. In a lot of ways, we all live in our own little 'cults', although it's fair to say that most of *our* cults are more socially acceptable than the ones that society points at because they challenge too many social niceties.

One of the most important things I have learned about social conditioning is the impact of what we are taught in our formative years. By this, I mean the way that we're conditioned about the things that are right and wrong, good and bad, acceptable and unacceptable and so on. These messages form our 'rules' for life and create an invisible platform for the direction we take moving forwards.

Initially, when we think about where those messages come from, we immediately think of our family: our parents, grandparents and siblings They usually form the closest orbit in the family cell, with ourselves at the nucleus, and in some ways have the greatest impact on our young lives. What we're usually less aware of are the hidden messages that target our subconscious and unconscious minds. These are the ones that really drive our behaviour and the way in which we act, react and think.

There are hidden messages in every area of our lives. We're taught to rely on community to survive, and it is from community that we're given strong lessons around the parts of ourselves that are accepted – and the parts that are less acceptable. As the people around us teach us those lessons, we shape ourselves to fit an image that we think others find acceptable. But what's really happening is that we become slaves to the judgement of the outside world, morphing and changing as the feedback demands.

As an overlay, we're bombarded with messages from advertising campaigns that target us in ways that trigger our behaviour and shape our mind around the things we 'must have' to be successful – to be *happy*. We see and hear messages around us all day long that tell us the ways in which we must try harder, so that we can achieve more. We spend countless hours and dollars in search of the next big thing that will make us a better person.

The consequence of all this 'noise' is that we're constantly and exhaustively searching *outside ourselves* for all our answers.

> *A big life lesson for me was in realising that so long as I was searching <u>externally</u> for my answers, I was always going to come up short.*

For decades, I shaped and moulded myself into a form that I believed the world would find acceptable. I punished, criticised and chastised myself relentlessly, because I couldn't ever reach the unattainable goals that I set for myself. Whilst I lived in this space and with this mindset, I was forever hiding away the parts of myself that I thought others found unacceptable. Eventually, this created an empty space within myself.

That empty space within drove me to give more of myself, to be of more service and to be a 'better' person – all in a desperate bid to fill that space and be whole again. What I didn't realise was that on my quest to be a better person, my conditioning was only allowing me to look for and learn from the people, activities and things that I had been taught were 'acceptable'.

What I actually needed to do was to pull out those pieces of myself that I had hidden away and learn to love them again. But like everyone else, I was so enmeshed in my 'normal' way of living that I was blind to how badly I needed to do this work. And worse, I had mastered living with the empty space within, so I was very adept at convincing myself that everything would be okay. In short, I was too strong for 'little thoughts' to prompt me to take action.

So, when I experienced my breakdown I suddenly had nothing to do, nowhere to go and no one to answer to. There was only one thing in front of me to focus on: myself. I no longer had a choice whether or not to look at these pieces; the catalyst for action had arrived with a bang – almost a literal one.

The journey back to being whole could only be completed once I'd looked at all the pieces and decided which ones I did – and didn't – want to take forward with me.

Looking at *all* the pieces of yourself and loving them without *judgement* is a very difficult thing to do, particularly when you've

been trained by the world around you that there are parts of yourself that are bad. It's completely overwhelming and, initially at least, it seems impossible to do. It's so much harder when you are on your knees and unable to get back up, having pushed yourself to the wall and come to a crashing halt.

The only way through this was to take a deep breath and look at each piece, one at a time; anything else was just too overwhelming and traumatic, enough to bring the whole process to a standstill.

One step at a time, I picked up each piece of myself and looked it in the eye. As I looked at each piece, I started to understand the power of the language that we use, and the distinct lack of self-compassion that I had in my life.

Along the way, I had internalised a number of beliefs: *'Doing anything for myself is being selfish'*.

Or this one: *'Allowing myself any acknowledgment of my strengths and talents is just showing off'*.

And my personal favourite: *'Taking a rest is the same thing as giving up'*.

I had become so harsh with myself that I allowed myself no space to breathe – it had become completely untenable for me to continue living this way. It was little wonder that my body and mind gave in and forced me to stop.

As I became more aware of the hidden rules, messages and things I had locked away inside myself, it became clearer to me that I needed to turn my focus *inwards* to find my answers. I started thinking about ways that I could more easily find the hidden things that I had created and stored in my subconscious and unconscious minds. Eventually, I created a process that I called 'getting curious with life' that allowed me to introduce a questioning mind into my everyday life.

The most important part of this process was creating a system that allowed me to stop the auto-pilot part of my brain from automatically kicking in and making all my decisions for me. To do this, I started asking myself a question any time someone told me something – particularly if they told me that I 'had to' do something.

For example, I started to notice things that were being said in some of the gym classes I was attending. One day the instructor in my cycle class shouted: *'Push yourself harder – make it count!'* I found myself answering this statement in my head with: *'Surely it counts because I came to class today!'*

Another example is when Easter time rolls around and all of a sudden, all the gym instructors start telling you that you have to push yourself harder so you can burn more calories – because it's Easter time and therefore you must have overindulged on chocolate, right? I would find myself thinking: *'Whoever said that just because it's Easter you have to overindulge? And even if you do, where is it written that you have to punish yourself for it?'*

I started to notice all the hidden messages in the marketing that was appearing around me – and I suddenly understood why our society has moved to such a materialistic, immediate-need environment.

One of the biggest impacts of my experience with a breakdown was that I couldn't stand anything other than the basics of life around me – right down to the food I ate, the things I could tolerate watching on TV, the books I read and so on. I found it very hard to concentrate because my mind couldn't focus, and I couldn't watch anything on TV that was violent, malicious or nasty in any way. Even whilst watching bland TV programs, I had to play games on my iPad at the same time because it provided me with a 'buffer' so that I couldn't feel any emotional connection with what I was seeing.

The benefit of this was that I was distant and disconnected from the marketing that was going on around me. I was no longer hooked into being triggered by an advertisement telling me and showing me all the things I must have now to fill the void inside me and make me happy.

I wasn't a massive shopper before my breakdown, but I also wasn't consciously connected with the things I did buy. I bought without much thought as to whether I needed the thing I was buying. More importantly, I had no thought for the impact on the environment or myself. So, finding myself in a very vulnerable position where anything other than the basics created a big impact, I started learning about the toxic load in our lives and the effect on the world around us.

I became very conscious of my own impact on the world, but also of the impact I had on myself, and I began to introduce easy and simple ways to embrace and embed self-compassion. Again, I overlaid the 'getting curious with life' point-of-view and I started looking at why I was making some of the choices I had been making.

Most of my answers came down to one of two things: either I had not taken the time to educate myself with enough knowledge about the things I was buying, or I did not value myself highly enough (that is, I wasn't worthy enough) to make a different decision.

A classic example of this occurred repeatedly while my husband, Jon, was away on work trips. On those occasions I didn't bother worrying about what I ate – or if I even ate at all. When I looked at this more closely – and actually called it out as an unhealthy behaviour – I realised that I didn't believe that I was worth the effort of putting something nutritious together, just for myself. I am a really creative and talented home cook and I absolutely infuse my food creations with love, but somehow, I had created a belief that I wasn't worthy of receiving any of that beautiful food if there was no one else around to create it for in the first place. In other words, I was invisible when it came to cooking.

Realising some of these things gave me big 'ah-ha' moments which was great – but then I needed to work out how I could do things differently so that I could reduce the impact and reverse the effects of the beliefs I had found.

When people come to work with me, one of the most common things they tell me they want to get out of the process is to have more clarity in their lives. When someone feels lost in life, a part of what's going on is a lack of direction, with no real way of knowing which way to turn or where to source the answers from.

It certainly was for me, although heightened in a lot of ways because everything in my life had collapsed when I hit the wall and there wasn't any focal point from which I could start. I started to ask myself a simple set of questions that helped me to separate the things I needed to have a look at from the things that weren't relevant to me.

The first question I asked was this: *'Is what I am being told relevant to me?'*

The purpose of asking this question was to create a space between what I was being told and my reaction. This was critical, because it was the one thing that allowed me to stop my auto-pilot from taking over. Asking this question provided me with time to consciously respond to what was happening in my life, rather than having my subconscious making my decisions for me. This question alone gave me a connection to my life which allowed me to actually start living in the present moment.

As I asked this question, I noticed that I would get either a 'yes' or a 'no' answer in my head, so I started to tune in more closely to the answers I was getting. I decided to play a little game for a day and follow the answers in my head to see what would happen.

If I got an answer of 'yes' then I would ask myself some more questions – things like *'what else do I need to know about this?'*, or *'what do I believe about this?'* – so that I could start exploring the hidden messaging that might be tucked away in my subconscious mind.

The more I followed the answers that I received through playing this game, the more I noticed that my life was moving in an effortless flow. In essence, the more I got curious about my own life, the more of my own answers I found. And at last, the more I felt my life was 'flowing', the smaller the void within me became. It suddenly occurred to me that by moving my focus within and re-shaping some beliefs that were working against me, I was finally able to start filling the empty space that had driven me to exhaustion for decades.

Not only that, I also realised that by introducing a habit of asking myself some simple, easy questions, I had also created a process that allowed me to effortlessly introduce change into my life with ease and grace.

In fact, this process was so easy that it didn't even feel like anything had changed. I simply asked a few questions that allowed me to look at things in a different way and then make a conscious decision about how I wanted to interact with those things moving forwards.

NUFFdoms

Throughout our lives we are constantly told by people what we 'have to do', 'should do' and who we 'should be'. We become so adept at living under the demands of those around us that we forget that we have free will in our own lives, and that we can make our own decisions.

In the early years of our life we may have experienced uncomfortable – and sometimes even painful – feedback about who we are and the way we have chosen to do things. This usually leads us to behave in a way that we think people around us will accept. Often we allow ourselves to become so afraid of stepping out of line that we become stuck; frozen in our ability to easily make choices that create the best life for ourselves.

If it's time to start to do things a little bit differently for yourself, then here's a simple and practical exercise that might help you to choose a slightly different path for yourself:

1. When you hear the words 'you have to' or 'you should', teach yourself to stop and before you respond, ask yourself the following question: *'is this right for me?'*

    You will get either a 'Yes' or 'No' answer in your head.

    _____

    _____

    _____

    _____

2. If you get the answer 'Yes', write down how all the ways that this helps you to align with your values:

    _____

    _____

    _____

    _____

3. If the answer is 'No', is there a different/similar thing that might be a better fit for what is being suggested to you?

___

4. If you decide to go ahead with the suggestion, what is the easiest, simplest and kindest way for you to bring this thing into your life?

___

THE ECONOMY OF ENOUGH - *UNLOCKING THE SECRET TO HAPPILY EVER AFTER*

Notes

CHAPTER 12

"The world as we have created it is a process of our thinking. It cannot be changed without changing our thinking."

– Albert Einstein

The Other Side of Change

There's a pattern that is embedded in almost everyone that is raised in a first world environment, particularly if they are female: *to be less than you were born to be.*

The early childhood years – roughly from birth to seven years of age – are where you form the basis and the rules for the foundations that will govern the way you live your life. For almost everyone, the life messaging you are taught during these formative years will determine the way that you will see the world as you move forwards. These life messages will be wholly dependent upon the unique combination of people, places and things that are in your life as you grow up.

As you grow and develop, you take on board that unique set of circumstances presented to you and filter them through your memory bank of experiences. This, in turn, creates an outcome for you in your mind, which then kicks into gear and computes the best result that it can see for you. Finally, acting on auto pilot, you morph and shape yourself to create the best result for the situation.

As a young child, you learn to create the version of yourself that is acceptable to the world around you, by taking your cue from the feedback that is given to you. When you do something that is good or acceptable, you are rewarded, praised, loved and included. When you do something that is bad or unacceptable, you are punished, criticised, scorned and excluded.

The pain you feel when you do something wrong is often so severe that you create a filter for yourself that ensures you do not 'wrong' anyone again. Conversely, when you do something that is good there is a sense of relief that you are out of the firing line for a small piece of time. Yes, that's right – even when it's a good result we still find a way to frame it as being the avoidance of a negative situation instead of simply embracing it as a positive.

It is important to stop and note that the sense of relief from being judged as having done something right, contrasted with the pain of the judgement attached to doing something wrong, are poles apart in terms of the way we experience them.

I'll bet if you were asked to stop right now and write down the times that you were punished for having done something 'wrong', you could remember lots of occasions: like the time where you felt the pain of stepping on someone's toes, or of being told that there was something about yourself that someone else had publicly pointed out as somehow being 'not right'.

I am also willing to bet that there will be fewer things you could remember if you had to write down the times that you had received positive feedback about things that were good or right.

I certainly remember times when I was exuberant when talking to someone, or having fun with friends, and I was told to 'stop showing off'. Or, when I was chosen for a lead role in a school play and the other kids said that 'I was only chosen because I was the teacher's pet'. Or when I was chosen to be the school captain of a sport, and others said that it 'wasn't fair that I was picked again'.

All of those moments are clear as a bell in my memory, because they were all associated with the pain of being on the receiving end of harsh and often nasty comments. They were also associated with the pain of slicing away pieces of myself that I had been taught were not 'good' aspects – and therefore were parts that needed to be hidden.

They should have been 'red letter' moments of joy, satisfaction and excitement but, sadly, that was not my experience.

In those moments, when other people gave me critical feedback, I wanted to shrivel up and make myself as small as I could, so that I could not only lessen the pain, but also limit the chances of being picked on again at a later time. For me, those situations were things to be avoided at all costs, and my survival became about making myself the smallest version I could be so that I would not impact anyone around me.

When you struggle with being not good enough, you start to hang on every word that is sent your way. You scour the comments for information about whether or not you're presenting an acceptable façade. Every piece of external feedback then supplies one of your inner demons with fodder that keeps the negative conversation going, until you're not only dealing with the criticism from the outside world but also an internal battle that is being waged to slowly decimate the self.

After pushing myself to the brink of death and then starting to put myself back together, I experienced a few home truths about the ways in which I had allowed myself to stray from the core of who *I am* as a unique human being.

The first of these truths was the realisation that I had conditioned myself so strongly to avoid the pain of being judged that I had become extraordinarily afraid of change. Change had become synonymous with being in the firing line. In fact, that scenario was so embedded within me – and completely associated with nerve-shredding pain – that it overrode everything I knew about dealing with the world. To me, it felt like taking the risk of stepping in *any direction* would put me in that firing line, a fate more excruciating than death.

The second of these truths was this: constantly moving toward the 'rewards' of doing the 'right' things added absolutely nothing to my happiness, and simply left me feeling numb. This was a big 'light bulb' moment for me, because I could suddenly and very clearly see that

even though I had spent my entire life doing everything to please everyone around me, there was no joy, laughter or happiness in my life.

I had been feeding my internal battle with the opinions of others. To make matters worse, those opinions were based on a *sliver* of information about me, but I consumed that sliver as a *whole truth*. I didn't realise that by engaging in this behaviour, I was handing over responsibility for my wellbeing, growth and development to sources external to me. Because I did this unconsciously, I had no idea that my very direction in life was being controlled by people over whom I had no control – their actions, thoughts, reactions or behaviour. I spent my entire life living on tenterhooks, desperately worried about their responses and constantly walking on egg shells trying to keep everything calm and on level.

Doing the 'right' thing according to everyone else simply gave me a false sense of safety.

With the rise in technology and the advent of the highly visible life that we all now lead – thanks to our interactions via social media – the fear of the pain that comes with stepping out of line and doing something 'wrong' is so intensely heightened that it has now moved to being a full-blown fear of change.

Now, if we do something wrong it can be broadcast globally with the touch of just one person's finger on a button. So, that sliver of information can be sent out through the airwaves and can reach millions of people whose opinions then weigh heavily on us, despite the fact that we don't even know them, and more importantly, *they don't even really know us.*

Very few of us take any time to consider whether what we have read or seen is real, or whether it is true, in part or even at all. Instead, we simply react, just the way we have been taught to, and launch with our own opinion (and outrage, at times), and simply add to the growing pile of social commentary. Public criticism in an open forum has also now moved to a state of nasty and sometimes venomous critique, with very little thought for the impact on the *human being* that is on the receiving end.

We shove more of ourselves away, into the darkness where no one can see, so that there are less and less parts of ourselves that are open to criticism from others. Controversial things that we might be willing to discuss with a small number of people in a face-to-face format are things we avoid like the plague in social media, because we've seen how quickly a seemingly innocent conversation can spiral out of control *in seconds*.

In this environment, our conditioning accelerates and our fear of the pain that is associated with public shaming is heightened. We become frozen puppets, stuck in a life that others have created for us, and squashed into a shape that is foreign to us, extremely uncomfortable and less and less likely to serve us the longer we remain unmoving and in place. We ultimately become immobilised by this fear.

Understanding the role that fear plays in life was something that I uncovered in the search for myself. Because I was locked in a story that 'life had to be hard', it was a painful lesson for me to learn. However, eventually I was able to understand that my fear of change was nothing more than a distraction that was stopping me from taking the steps that led me to the bigger and better things waiting for me.

Perhaps my biggest 'light bulb' moment around all of this came when I realised that our fear around change has such an intense hold over us simply because we've lost sight of who we are – and now we're so conditioned that it feels like it's too hard to find out. We've been told for so long what is right and wrong, good and bad, acceptable and not, that we're too scared to think for ourselves and we've lost sight of the things that are important to us.

One of the first things I do when I start to work with someone in a one-on-one format is to ask them to tell me what their values are. This is almost always met by a blank stare, followed by a brief flare of panic at being asked a question they can't answer, and then followed up with a heavy confession that they don't know.

We have allowed ourselves to be so thrown around by the weight of others' opinions that we have become completely lost in the search for the truth in our lives. When we're living the lives that other people have given us, we can't align ourselves to the things that are actually worthwhile to us. What we don't realise is that it is only when we step into this alignment that we can find the flow that is uniquely related to our being able to master our own lessons with ease and grace.

Intuitively, we all know when we hear something that is true – it's a feeling that we get that allows us to resonate completely with what we've heard or seen. What most of us aren't taught is that our biggest challenge isn't in being able to know the truth; rather, it's to be able to respond to that truth with a *conscious* thought rather than suppressing it because it's too scary to look at.

Why? Well, because we've been taught to be so unconscious in our actions. We allow that auto-pilot function to kick in, and we respond in the way we've been conditioned to.

One of the biggest differences in my life post-recovery is that I have taught myself to stop and listen when I uncover something that is a truth for me. It's also taught me to get curious about my own life and allow my mind to create questions that will uncover hidden patterns for me. I ask myself simple questions that allow me to uncover as much about the truth as possible and, most importantly, I allow whatever the answer is to hold its own ground.

By this, I mean that I don't start to create reasons why the answer is good or bad; I simply allow the answer to be exactly what it is. For example, the uncovered truth might be about a pattern that I have identified as recurring through my life. The question I ask about this pattern might be something like this: *'Has repeating this pattern worked for me so far?'* The answer to this question will either be 'yes' or 'no'.

If the answer is 'no', the temptation is to then start being hard on yourself for allowing that pattern to impact your life for so long. Instead, I allow the answer of 'no' to stand on its own two feet and then adopt a mindset of *'that's interesting, I wonder how that pattern came about in the first instance?'* This helps to turn an emotionally-charged answer into something to be analysed or reviewed objectively.

Working with information in this way allows me to reduce the emotional response that is attached to my thoughts. When I can reduce the emotion, I can gain so much more clarity about a situation. It also allows me to be very present with what is happening in my life. The ability to be present means that I can make conscious decisions *in the moment* about what I would like to happen next, and this then shuts down any power that not being good enough might have had in the situation.

In short, I take away all the wriggle room that 'enough' might have previously been able to use to get a grip on different situations in my life.

By changing the emotional relationship I have with change, I have been able to move to a place where I can deliberately step into change and experience it as fun. I made the conscious decision to relate to change with ease and grace, rather than allow its grip to control me through fear. This simple decision alone has made it really easy for me to ebb and flow with whatever happens in every day, and it has rewarded me with the realisation that my life was waiting for me to simply step up and start living it.

NUFFdoms

At different times in our lives we're taught to hide parts of ourselves because someone around us has told us that there is something about us that they don't like. Whether this happens through direct or subtle feedback it leaves us feeling bad about ourselves, and the only way we're taught to combat that pain is by turning away from pieces of ourselves that allow us to be whole.

The following exercise is a really simple way to start the process of finding those pieces of ourselves that we've hidden away. Until we find the pieces, shower them with love and allow them to reintegrate, it can be really hard for us to be whole again.

1. Think about an area of your life where you know that you deliberately hold yourself back, or play small. (If you're struggling to think of anything, start with the things where you are really critical about yourself). Write about that area of your life below:

   _____
   _____
   _____
   _____
   _____

2. What benefit do you get from playing small in this area of your life? What are you creating a distraction from?

   _____
   _____
   _____
   _____
   _____

3. What are three simple things you could do to right now to allow yourself to step into your greatness in this area:

_____

_____

_____

_____

_____

4. Thinking about the first thing listed above, what are three simple things you could do to take the first step?

_____

_____

_____

_____

_____

5. Write down when and how you will take the first step listed in question 4:

_____

_____

_____

_____

_____

Notes

CHAPTER 13

"*We must be the change we want to see in the world.*"

– Mahatma Gandhi

Finding YOU

Without a doubt, the most confronting experience of my breakdown was looking in the mirror and not recognising the person that was looking back at me. Over time, I had strayed so far from my path, and for so long, that I didn't know who I was anymore.

When I experienced my breakdown, it was like being shattered into a million pieces and being unable to put them back together again. In hindsight, I know that this happened because the pieces didn't fit who I was, and I needed time and space to be able to re-construct my true self.

When I looked in the mirror, it reflected back to me visions of being lost, alone and extraordinarily fragile. I was in a very vulnerable state, and having my altered image add to an overwhelming sense of loss was a heavy burden to bear.

Being in such an extreme emotional state, I wasn't aware of it at the time, but I hadn't really looked at myself in the mirror – any mirror – for a very long time. Sure, I did my hair and makeup every day I went to work and probably checked my reflection a couple of times a day to make sure everything was in order, but I hadn't looked myself in the eyes and met my own gaze for decades – if ever.

Through my recovery, I learned to find the pieces of myself I needed to take forwards as well as how to create new pieces that would complete the 'puzzle' that was me. I also learned that it wasn't until I was able to define who I was that I was able to comfortably look into my own eyes and smile at my reflection.

I had pushed myself so hard, and for so long, by squashing myself into a format that I believed everyone around me needed. My body was screaming at me and I was in significant pain all the time. My mind was exhausted and constantly giving me signals that I needed to stop, but I refused to listen.

Eventually, there was no choice; I dropped so that I could be saved.

Throughout my life, one of my greatest strengths was always my ability to find a solution to someone else's problems, issues, situations or needs. So, when I experienced my breakdown, it was the first time in my life that I didn't know where to turn or which direction to go in. Previously, I would have simply clicked my fingers and a solution would be at hand. This time, however, I was staring at a blank space and seemingly had no capacity to cognitively work my way through the problem I was facing.

That situation continued until I discovered something vitally important: that the solutions I had created previously almost always involved me giving too much of myself, in order to make it easier for others in their lives. When you constantly give too much, logically there comes a time when there is nothing left to give.

Allowing others to experience and carry their own challenges was a big lesson for me to learn. I came to the realisation that by doing everything for everyone around me, I was not only adding significant pressure into my own life, but I was also taking away the ability for others to learn for themselves.

So, there I was, faced with an unintended consequence of my actions. Such a humbling realisation for a recovering perfectionist to have:

I had spent my life trying to take away others pain, only to realise that I had potentially hindered them more than I had helped them.

The good news from this was that I finally started to pay attention to the lessons being presented to me.

Forrest Gump may well have been taught that *'life is like a box of chocolates'*, but I believe that life is like an onion, filled with layers that peel back one at a time to teach us the lessons we need to learn.

Something I became all too familiar with was the same lesson appearing time and time again in my life. I would do the work, deal with the issue and move forward, only to have the same lesson appear again, as if through the back door.

I used to get really upset with myself and berate myself harshly because I clearly hadn't learned my lesson. Well, that's what I told myself, anyway. I was the toughest critic of my own development. It seemingly didn't matter what I had achieved, how much ground I had gained or how far forward I moved in my life – there was always something I found about myself to critique and to punish myself for.

I remember playing with a senior level netball team and our team was down by quite a few goals at three quarter time. I picked up my game and got intercept after intercept in the final quarter, which spurred the team to a win. After the game, everyone was congratulating me on how well I had played. My response was to immediately make myself small, and so I started telling the others about all the things I needed to work on to make myself a better player. I simply could not – would not – allow myself to acknowledge that I had played a great game.

My response to that game was reflective of every corner of my life. If someone complimented me on something, or congratulated me for doing something well, I would find a way to minimise their praise. It became completely ingrained in me to make sure that I presented as small a version of myself to the world as possible.

It wasn't until I collapsed and found myself with nothing else to do except sift through the pieces of myself on the floor – so I could put the real version of myself together – that I realised I had created a battle with 'enough' to ensure that I could never step into the greatest version of me. My battle with not being good enough was actually a highly effective distraction that kept me from growing and developing my talents to the extent they needed to be, in order for me to do the work I needed to be doing in the world.

Suddenly, this realisation gave me the clarity to understand that even at the depths of my struggle with 'enough', I shied away from the deep sense that I was meant to be doing something greater. I had no way of connecting with what that higher purpose was, and I was too afraid of what it might be, or what it might ask of me, to find out. I was frozen by the fear that I would be caught out for not being perfect – that somewhere, sometime, someone would point the finger at me and declare that I wasn't good enough to be doing what I was doing.

So, I played small. I lived my life with a focus of making sure that everyone around me was okay. I made sure that nothing I did would impact them in any way. I found ways to lift everyone around me, to make them feel better about themselves. I encouraged others to be the best version they could be.

> Meanwhile, I hid behind a façade of perfection and pretended that everything in my world was fine and dandy.

Like almost everyone I have met, I had proficiently mastered the art of being terrified of change. It's not surprising, then, that realising that I needed to change my life from one of complete service to others to a life that was more balanced – and included a focus on myself as well – was *completely overwhelming*.

I had decades of stories to unwind, and for someone who had so successfully presented a perfect disguise to the world for so long, it was terribly daunting to start to take steps into vulnerability and forge a life on a different path.

As I recovered, one small step at a time, I had to learn to reassimilate into the world, *as a very different person*. I was terrified of the judgement from others, particularly because my 'wound' was on the inside and couldn't be seen by anyone else. Mostly I was fragile, and with that fragility came a heightened fear that I had no idea where my future was going, what people would think of the new me and whether I could live up the expectations that others had of me.

I slowly stepped back into 'normal' life at the start of the moulding process that would eventually create a different person – a whole new and revised edition of myself. I was vulnerable and shaky, never knowing from day to day – and sometimes minute to minute – whether I would be okay. I had to learn to be in public and not worry if the people around me noticed that I started crying. I had to learn to breathe slowly when I started to panic if I lost sight of my husband, Jon. I had to learn that a step was a step, no matter the direction it was in. I had to learn to see the signs that my energy levels were drained. Mostly, I had to learn to fall in love with self-compassion.

The life I had been living was slowly killing me. It was full of stress, exhaustion and commitments that clashed with my personal values and voraciously drained energy from a tank that was already dry.

In hindsight, I know that there wasn't one area of my life that was just for me, that nourished my soul and allowed me to refuel my energy tanks.

I worked hard through my recovery to rebuild myself, and at times I was close to dropping from the sense of overwhelm and fear. Somewhere, deep within myself, there is a well of strength that comes to the surface and carries me forward when I have no idea how I will go on. Learning that this is a strength – and a weakness – has been one of the greatest lessons I have ever learned.

Making sure I set up a solid platform for my life became a high priority for me. My journey had taught me that the experience of enduring, and then recovering from, a breakdown was something I didn't ever want to do again. It therefore became critical for me to make sure that I rebuilt my life with a structure that would support whatever I chose to do moving forwards.

Once I committed to this rebuild, I determined that the first thing I needed to do was to work out the things that were important to me, the things that really mattered. Working out, defining and writing down my values was the first step in this process. Once in place, my values became the centre point of my life. They became the filter that I would use to make decisions about what I wanted to do, where I wanted to go and who I wanted to be working with.

I also made sure that I understood what I needed to be able to refuel my energy on a daily basis. Before collapsing, I knew that I was tired but I had no idea how critically dry my energy tank really was. It wasn't until I dropped and couldn't get back up that I realised just how close to the brink I really was, and it took me almost four years of work to get my energy levels back to an even keel.

It isn't until you experience fluctuating energy levels that you realise just how important good energy stores are to living a happy life. For four years, I didn't know from day to day what my energy levels would be like until I woke up. I would have days when it would be all I could do to drag myself to the couch. There were other days where I could go like the Energizer Bunny all day. In short, I was all over the place, and that made it hard to get anything done, and even harder to feel like I could commit myself to any work engagements – because I couldn't guarantee that I would have the energy I needed, when I needed it, to deliver on a contract.

Self-compassion became my saving grace. Mastering the art of self-compassion gave me the edge I needed to get myself through whatever situation I faced in each moment. I firmly believe that teaching myself to be as compassionate to myself as I would be to my best friend is the one thing that has enabled me to step away from my battle with not being good enough.

Stepping into a kinder, softer and more compassionate version of myself has allowed me the space to laugh when something goes wrong. And let's face it, as a recovering perfectionist, I'm perfectly okay with learning a few lessons along the way, even when there are others around to see them!

NUFFdoms

Most of us were never taught to identify our values – nor how important they are in assisting us to keep our lives aligned with who we truly are. Knowing what your values are, and having them clearly defined, allows you to stop and look at what is important to you as a unique individual.

Creating your values is really simple – follow this exercise and you'll create your own in no time:

1. Consider the following question: *'if you were told today that you had 4 months to live, what would you do differently with your life that you aren't doing now?'*

   _____

   _____

   _____

   _____

2. Now consider this:

   Fact: We all think we're invincible and that we've got all the time in the world.

   Fact: One day we're all going to die.

   Fact: None of us knows how much time we have left!

   Write down how these statements make you feel:

   _____

   _____

   _____

   _____

3. Ask yourself the following question: 'Am I doing what I want to be doing if this was the last day of *my life?*'

　

　

　

4. Given the above questions and answers, it becomes very important to start living our lives in line with the things that are important to us. Creating your values is as easy as completing the following table:

    ➤ Start by asking yourself these questions:
      o *'What is important in my life?'*
      o *'What do I truly value?'*
    ➤ Keep asking yourself these questions until you have written down 5 things.
    ➤ Use the notes column to add some additional words or a description for each value.

	Value	Notes	Hierarchy
1.			
2.			
3.			
4.			
5.			

    ➤ After all of the 5 values have been written down, have a look at your values and then order them in order of importance to you from 1 to 5 (where 1 is the most important of them).

5. Use this list of values to help you make decisions around opportunities, situations, people, places and things that come up in your life.

    ➤ For example, if someone asks you to do something for them you can look back over your values table and see whether what you are being asked to do matches the things that are important to you. If the answer is 'Yes' then you know it is something you would like to be doing. If the answer is 'No' then you know that it doesn't match what is important to you and it might be best if you don't get involved.

Notes

CHAPTER 14

"Don't make yourself small. Not for anyone.

*If someone tells you you're too much...
too loud, too sensitive, too fierce, too caring,
too intellectual, too optimistic, too realistic,
too logical, too emotional...
just smile and move on, my friend.*

Clearly, they aren't enough for you."

– L.R. Knost

The Economy of Enough

What is enough?

How do you know when you have enough of it?

So few of us have ever taken the time to think about what 'enough' actually means. We spend our lives locked in its tight grasp, struggling against the tide and trying to break free, only to be squeezed tighter and held firmly in place.

We're so engrossed in the battle that we've never stopped to wonder if there's another way that we could be living.

Two of the most common themes that I hear recurring in people's lives is that they feel lost and that they don't feel that their life has any purpose to it. Then they arrive on my doorstep because they're driven to try and make an impact in the world, but they feel like they're failing at every turn. These are all things that I completely understand – because I experienced them too.

I know, all too well, how unbearable the pain of living like this is, and I also understand how we came to believe that delaying change to the last minute was the easier path. But the last minute – that minute when you're desolate, almost inconsolable and when the pain is simply too great to bear any more – is actually *way more painful* than stepping forward and taking action now. We, all of us, know that we need to do *something*, but we've gotten ourselves so lost and confused that we simply cannot see that there is another way for us to live in the world.

There's a pattern that takes over life when 'enough' is in control. You find yourself constantly under pressure to deliver to everyone around you, whilst your mind is cruelly reminding you that everything you do is below standard, behind time or, worse still, a complete waste of time. You constantly feel like an abject failure. When others are around you, you always position yourself as lesser than them. You're constantly building them up, always pouring love, compassion and empathy their way and encouraging them to be the best version of themselves, whilst denying yourself the same simple courtesies for your own life.

The reality of this situation is that there is so much noise being created by what is going on around you that you can't see that you are stuck in a cycle of martyrdom. The power of the control that 'enough' holds over you is such that you constantly allow yourself to be and do things that drain your energy, that don't make you happy and that you most likely get very little enjoyment from. Your mind creates excuses for you about why you have to stay stuck in this way of living, and you speak the words of those excuses so often that you start to believe them.

> *Until you realise that the excuses are a distraction you've created so you don't have to own up to who you really are, you will remain enmeshed in the life you have given yourself.*

When you do finally realise that your reasons for doing what you've been doing are nothing more than excuses, and that you've been using them to hide behind – sometimes for decades – it can be very confronting. Fear starts to raise its voice and you can feel panic rising within you – because if they're just excuses, then that might mean you have to make some changes.

In version 1.0 of Bronwen, I hid from any thoughts that change might be needed. I hid by finding more things to heap onto my already overloaded schedule. Subconsciously I'd reasoned that the busier I was, the less time I had to think about whether or not I might have gotten my 'reasons' wrong.

In fact, I had wandered so far from myself that it seemed impossible for me to even look at how I might do some things differently, and because I was so hard on myself, it seemed that the only way to make some change would be to start everything over completely.

I didn't understand that I could make significant changes in my life by choosing to take just one small step differently. All of my life experience had been about struggle and misery. I had taken on board so much of other people's 'stuff' – and felt that I was responsible for the wellbeing and success of so many other people's lives – that I convinced myself that I had to keep going exactly as I was. I'd concluded that since my life was worth so much less than theirs, it was okay to sacrifice mine to save theirs. In this twisted way of thinking – not that I knew it was twisted at the time – I'd convinced myself that doing so might mean that at least I had served some purpose.

Yet despite my belief that I was here to serve others and having put myself in a position to be everyone else's sacrificial lamb, I was restless. My strength kept me in place and powering down a path that wasn't mine, yet I knew that I wasn't doing what I was supposed to be doing – that I wasn't fulfilling my purpose in life.

When I broke, I was forced to experience my entire life's emotions in a very short period of time. This was an extremely painful and confronting experience, but it has given me a clarity about life that I didn't have before. Now, it is easy for me to connect to and understand the emotions that I was experiencing at different stages of my life and to see the way that I can use those experiences to help me navigate my path forward.

I was fighting so many battles on so many fronts in my life, and all from an unconscious state of mind. There was so much happening, and all at the same time, but I was too busy saving the world to notice that I was simultaneously sending myself to oblivion. If you've ever used the function in a computer program that allows you to make an object transparent, then you'll get a great picture of what I was doing to

my life. The longer I stayed in this frame of mind, the more transparent I became until there was nothing of me left for the world to see.

I realised that I was fighting a war: a pitched battle between trying to keep myself small enough, so as to not impact everyone else, whilst at the same time clinging on with my fingertips to hold my place in the world. Once I understood this, I let go and allowed the war to come to an end. I dispensed with my need to hide, my mission to dim my own light and make sure everyone around me was okay. I was done with 'enough'.

I still carry an incredible amount of empathy for others, but I view this empathy in another way now. Instead of trying to fix everyone and give everything of myself to make sure that they are okay, I now simply smile at them and send them unconditional love, and a wish that all may work out in their world. I no longer need to step in and come to everyone's aid, because I now understand that allowing others to process their own 'stuff' and learn their own lessons is one of the greatest gifts I can give to them.

I've worked out how to connect to my individual power sources so that I can work in unison with the Universe to make empowered decisions for my life. I don't need to know all the ins and outs of every situation to be able to move forwards. I simply need to understand whether what is in front of me is something that is aligned with my values, or not. If not, then I let it go on its way to carry on its own journey. If yes, then I take steps to understand more.

I no longer yearn for simpler times like when I was younger – when life was easier, and I could escape to the countryside with my animals – because I no longer feel the need to escape from my own life. I not only understand what I am doing, but I also consciously know why I am doing it. This single premise is perhaps the most powerful thing I have introduced into the life of Bronwen 2.0.

None of this means that I no longer have challenges in my life – far from it. Of course, I still have things to grapple with; after all, I'm human and there is still so much for me to learn. In fact, in some ways I would say that my challenges come to me more quickly now.

The difference this time around is that I now understand that the challenges are nothing more than a sign for me to stop and take note, that there is something there for me to learn. Being able to view the challenges in this way makes it easy for me to live my life with ease and grace, and it also makes it easier for me to transition through the challenges in a very simple way.

'Enough' is no longer anything more or less than *enough*. It's simply a word to me now – and one that has no power or control over my life. I choose to view 'enough' as its own economy – the most powerful economy in the world.

Just like money, 'enough' can make you feel the euphoria of having lots of it, just as easily as it can bring you to your knees and make you feel the desolation of having none. 'Enough' can also come and go in a similar way to money. You can give too much of it and not take any in return, and you can make someone's day when you give them the gift of 'enough'.

I've experienced both ends of the spectrum in the economy of enough and I know where I would much rather spend my time. I've discovered that the quickest and most sure-fire way of getting to a constant place of being more than enough is this: to make sure that I am the kindest person to myself in my life.

The journey to enough can only be reached through self-compassion.

I once heard a talk-back segment on the radio where the host of the show was asking callers to phone in and tell them what they wish could be brought back from the 1980s. One lady phoned in and said that she would like to see '...*manners and compassion for other human beings...*' brought back.

Whilst I understand the sentiment of this statement, the reality is that times have changed. Life travels in a different way and at a different speed now. We might not be able to turn the clock back, or influence the speed of life, but what we can do is take back responsibility for ourselves. We have to find the way for ourselves that allows us to remain connected and conscious despite what is going on around us.

If you want to see more manners around you, then have better manners yourself. If you want people to be more compassionate, then be more compassionate yourself. The world is but a mirror reflecting back the things that are important to us. Instead of getting ourselves all worked up over the things that other people are doing, use the mirror to guide you to the lessons you need to learn, and to be able to see where your values are in alignment. If you spend more time moving in the directions where you see your values reflected, you will more easily find your pathway in life.

I'm no longer interested in whether or not I'm good enough, or even whether I am worthy. I'm not swayed by, or even curious about, what other people think about what I'm doing, or how I'm doing it. I simply make a promise to myself every day that I will do the best that I can with whatever I have chosen to do in that moment.

I'm content to leave others to their own decisions for their own lives and feel that I am blessed to be so consciously connected with the decisions I make for mine. I am absolutely loving being able to explore new and interesting places and concepts, and more and more I am meeting people who challenge my mindset in the most loving and generous ways.

Life is an adventure, with twists and turns, opportunities and – most importantly – possibilities. I have found the way to set myself free to stand strongly, step boldly and dream without limits.

If you haven't already done so, now is the time for you to join me, and then maybe you can dream without limits too.

NUFFdoms

Enough can wreak havoc in our lives – when we let it. Until you learn to look at yourself through a filter of love, it can be very difficult to see that you are a divine being on an adventure, experiencing everything there is to experience in a human lifetime.

Ignore the critics and find your rose-coloured glasses – put them on and see yourself in all your greatness.

If I had read those two paragraphs whilst enmeshed in the biggest struggle of my life, I would have been completely lost as to where to start to be able to achieve this. It's actually really simple – here's how:

1. What is the kindest definition of 'enough' that you can create?

    This is your opportunity to create a definition of 'enough' that you can use from this point forwards to drive your life in a different way.

    Write *YOUR* new defintion of enough below:

    _____
    _____
    _____
    _____
    _____
    _____
    _____
    _____
    _____
    _____

2. When and how will you apply your new definition of enough in your life?

   Write down when you think that you will need this defition of enough, and when you do need it, how will you allow yourself to apply it?

   _____
   _____
   _____
   _____
   _____
   _____
   _____
   _____
   _____
   _____

3. If you have situations where you apply this definition and find that you haven't quite achieved 'enough', how will work with yourself so that you can do things a little bit differently moving forwards?

   _____
   _____
   _____
   _____
   _____
   _____
   _____
   _____
   _____
   _____

4. When and how often will you actively reflect on whether your new definition of 'enough' is working for you, and supporting you moving forwards?

_____
_____
_____
_____
_____
_____

Notes

_____
_____
_____
_____
_____
_____
_____
_____
_____
_____
_____
_____
_____

CHAPTER 15

Namaste

*My soul honours your soul.
I honour the place in you where the entire
Universe resides.
I honour the light, love, truth, beauty & peace
within you, because it is also within me.
In sharing these things, we are united, we are the same.
We are one.*

Conclusion

If you had told me a few short years ago that I would be writing a book about the impact of allowing not being good enough to run riot in your life, I would have laughed and thought you were making fun of me. That was the sum total of where I thought my worth was in the world – to be the butt of other people's jokes.

To look at me, you would never have guessed that I was stuck in a spiral of low self-esteem, and with so little self-worth that it was impossible for me to see that I was the best person to write about how it feels to be controlled by a nemesis that is all encompassing, all demanding and wholly supressing.

I had created a place for myself where I believed that I was put on this Earth to serve, and that my sole purpose was to make sure everyone around me was okay. If that meant that people made fun of me, even though it hurt me, surely that meant that I had served to make their day better. I was desperately unhappy, on my way to being significantly unwell and my life was spinning out of control.

Even though the responsibilities in my life were completely overwhelming, I couldn't completely shut out the thought that there must be more to life. Deep down, I knew that I was made for something more than what I was doing. I tried to hide from it, but I knew that somewhere along the way I had taken a turn down a path that didn't serve me and that I was no longer on my own path in life. Despite knowing this, I was too afraid to step out of the lane I had been given, so I gathered my strength, closed my mind and chose to soldier on, to push through and to 'just get to the other side' of the next crisis at hand.

My life lurched from one stressful situation to another – if it wasn't the impact of some work issue then it was something at home – and all of the pain was shoved into dark recesses within, hidden behind a calm, serene façade that portrayed success and happiness.

Eventually, there was too much pain shoved into too few spaces and it could no longer be contained within my physical form. The pain exploded, my world collapsed, and I was forced to stop, sit still and listen.

And listen I did. I retreated from the world so that I had the space to listen to the pain that was finally allowed out into the light of day. I listened as the pain told me the story of all the ways that I had diminished myself to make others around me feel alright. I listened to my heart as it requested the opportunity to experience life with love, ease and grace.

The more I listened, the more I knew that I had to do things differently. I realised that I was at a crossroads in my life – that I could return to my life as I knew it and keep walking the path to an early grave, or I could take small steps, albeit on very shaky legs, and choose to start walking in a different direction.

I chose to learn more about living life differently. I began to understand that I had the choice to apply a different filter in the way I looked at things – that I could allow myself to experience a life with peace and calm rather than tumult and grief.

I started to take small steps to explore ideas and information that I had previously closed my mind to, things that I had shied away from

because others didn't believe or might disapprove. For the first time, I started to experience what it was like to walk in my own shoes.

I've learned a lot in the ensuing years – first, in putting myself back together in version 2.0, and then later on, in making a commitment to myself to be open to receive the information I need, exactly when I need it. I also always ask that the information be received with ease and grace.

I'm not afraid to know who I am anymore. I know that I am worthy, so I no longer question it. I know that I am more than enough to easily achieve my purpose in life.

Not being good enough is no longer a foe. Now it's a warm and caring companion that simply helps me be conscious enough to notice the things around me. Enough no longer has any power over me. I find myself wanting to learn, wanting to explore, and I want to expand myself to the greatest depths and the farthest reaches so that I can be the greatest possible version of myself.

Arriving at this place within myself has taught me how to connect with my own answers and has allowed me to find peace and happiness in every moment of my life. The struggle is gone, and I finally understand what it means to surrender the need to control every second.

There is only one direction in life that allows you to live in a way that unleashes your potential. You are the only one who knows what that direction is for you.

So be brave, be strong, be loyal, be fun – be whoever you know yourself to truly be. Find the pathway that allows you to walk easily, and always allow yourself to walk with the greatest of self-compassion.

The world is waiting for you to become the magnificent person you were always supposed to become.

You are enough. You are brilliant. Let yourself shine.

Namaste.

Contact Details

To book Bronwen Sciortino for a keynote presentation,
half or full day workshop nationally or internationally, please contact:

Bronwen Sciortino
sheIQ Life
PO Box 65
Melville, WA 6956

Ph: +61 438 624 868
E: info@sheiqlife.com
W: www.sheiqlife.com

Facebook: www.facebook.com/bronwensciortinoauthor
Instagram: www.instagram.com/bronwensciortino_author
Linkedin: https://au.linkedin.com/in/bronwensciortino

References

I have been very privileged to access a host of resources that have helped shape the path that I now travel. Following are a list of resources that have helped me put this book together:

- Philip K. Dick — *An American writer known for his work in science fiction. His work explored philosophical, social, and political themes, with stories dominated by monopolistic corporations, alternative universes, authoritarian governments, and altered states of consciousness*
- Charles Dickens — *Renowned author of many bestselling books, including the famous 'Great Expectations'.*
- Sylvia Plath — *Sylvia Plath was a gifted and troubled poet, known for the confessional style of her work. Her interest in writing emerged at an early age, and she started out by keeping a journal.*
- Paulo Coelho — *Paulo Coelho de Souza is a Brazilian lyricist and novelist. He is best known for his novel The Alchemist*
- David Bottoms — *Is the author of eight other books of poetry, In a U-Haul North of Damascus, Under the Vulture-Tree, Armored Hearts: Selected and New Poems[1], Vagrant Grace[2], Oglethorpe's Dream, Waltzing Through the Endtime[3], and We Almost Disappear[4] as well as two novels,*
- C.S. Lewis — *C.S. Lewis was a British writer and lay theologian. He held academic positions in English literature at both Oxford University and Cambridge University. He is best known for his works of fiction, especially The Screwtape Letters, The Chronicles of Narnia, and The Space Trilogy.*
- Steve Maraboli — *Steve Maraboli is a life-changing Speaker, bestselling Author, and Behavioral Scientist who lends his popular voice to various topics and has been dubbed by Inc. Magazine as, "The Most Quoted Man Alive ..."*
- George Orwell — *Eric Arthur Blair (25 June 1903 – 21 January 1950), better known by his pen name George Orwell, was an English novelist, essayist, journalist and critic whose work is marked by lucid prose, awareness of social injustice, opposition to totalitarianism and outspoken support of democratic socialism.*
- Oprah Winfrey — *Oprah Winfrey is an American media executive, actress, talk show host, television producer and philanthropist. She is best known for her talk show The Oprah Winfrey Show, which was the highest-rated television program of its kind in history and was nationally syndicated from 1986 to 2011 in Chicago.*
- Alan W. Watts — *Alan Wilson Watts was a British philosopher who interpreted and popularised Eastern philosophy for a Western audience.*
- Albert Einstein — *Albert Einstein was a German-born theoretical physicist who developed the theory of relativity, one of the two pillars of modern physics. His work is also known for its influence on the philosophy of science. He is best known to the general public for his mass–energy equivalence formula $E = mc^2$, which has been dubbed "the world's most famous equation".*
- Mahatma Gandhi — *Mohandas Karamchand Gandhi was an Indian activist who was the leader of the Indian independence movement against British rule. Employing nonviolent civil disobedience, Gandhi led India to independence and inspired movements for civil rights and freedom across the world.*
- L.R. Knost — *Award-winning author, feminist, and social justice activist, L.R.Knost, is the founder and director of the children's rights advocacy and family consulting group, Little Hearts/Gentle Parenting Resources, and Editor-in-Chief of Holistic Parenting Magazine*
- Namaste — *Namaste, sometimes spoken as Namaskar, Namaskaram is a respectful form of greeting in Hindu custom, found on the Indian subcontinent mainly in India and Nepal and among the Indian diaspora.*

I am grateful for the wisdom and knowledge that each and every one of these resources has brought to my life and my writing.

Thank you

My time writing this book was very special – it flowed through me with an integrity and a magic that I've never felt before. I'm completely supported in my journey and I am thankful for the love, encouragement and support of so many significant people:

- Jon Sciortino – my # 1 fan – you've always got my back, talking me up to anyone that will listen. You keep it real for me, you love me and support me unconditionally – no matter where I find my journey taking me.

- To my awesome friends – Sharon Marsden, Karen & Andre Clay, Pippa Young and Catherine Rapley – no matter how far apart we are or how seldom we get to see each other, we pick up exactly where we left off – like there has been no time passed. You are all of you invaluable to me and I love you with all of my heart.

- Melaney Ryan – your generosity in sharing your wisdom and knowledge and your continual support mean the world to me. Mahatma and so much love.

- Freya Sampson – we've just found each other again – thank you for the lifetimes of fun and adventure – may we have many, many more!

- Jessica Zaccaria – thank you for your fabulous editing skills – as a recovering perfectionist it is always daunting for me to hand my work over for critique by someone else and I sincerely thank you for your love and kindness in your review. Thank you.

- Kelsey Allen – my typesetter and friend – your support, enthusiasm and genuine love of all of my achievements is something I treasure.

- Dale Simmonds – my designer and illustrator – somehow you take my words and create a visual world for them – it is an absolute privilege watching my work merge with yours. Thank you once again for your creations.

- Thank you to each and every one of my readers – your support over my journey, your words of love, testimonials, reviews and connection through the social media world mean so much to me.

I count myself very fortunate to have all of you in my world – each and every day.

Much love and may you all be inspired to step into your greatness so we can collectively create a magnificent world.

Other publications by Bronwen Sciortino

Keep It Super Simple

Reducing Stress and Increasing Resilience, a brilliant guide to overcoming overwhelm, 'Keep It Super Simple' is the book you didn't know you needed!

When it comes to creating a simpler life there's many things that can impact you. This highly engaging book by award-winning business woman and author, Bronwen Sciortino, offers a brilliantly simple approach to overcoming overwhelm and living a life with less stress and more resilience.

Described as 'chocolate for your soul' ... 'Keep It Super Simple' shows you how to:

- live life differently every day because in a world wher e you lead a life filled with stress and exhaustion, you're robbing yourself of a fulfilled, healthy and happier life;
- find the best ways to recharge YOUR energy so you can stop being exhausted all the time;
- understand the importance of creating your values, how to align your life to them & live every day being true to you so you can bring your life into flow, bringing an ease and effortlessness you'll absolutely love;
- minimise the impact of FOMO & YOLO on your life which means you consciously choose the things you love doing rather than spending your life doing the things others tell you that you 'should' be doing;
- create the simple and practical steps that help make sure you're doing the things that are aligned with who you are, replacing the time and energy you have been putting into trying to be someone or something else with more rewarding ways of living and being;
- step away from stress & live a life that is calm & full of energy;
- easily implement simple steps that empower you in YOUR life – leading you to experience greater confidence and self integrity;
- have the confidence that there IS light at the end of the tunnel and that you are not stuck living a life someone else has given you;
- be yourself whilst limiting the impact of shame, guilt & recriminations from others;
- understand YOUR path to success so you can boldly step into the thick of YOUR life;

This book easily fits in your bag so you can easily take it with you everywhere you go, which means it'll be there as a support anytime you need it; AND it's in a workbook style, offering space for journaling and recording your 'Ah-ha' moments – deepening your understanding and ability to implement the new learning into your life. You can build on your thoughts, comments & feelings – almost like a diary which means you'll ne v er lose the important nuggets that will help you to move forward in your life.

Don't be surprised when you turn this into a reference for every day situations – it's likely to become a reflection tool that teaches you to make your own choices and guide your life as you learn to find your path forward.

Notes

www.ingramcontent.com/pod-product-compliance
Lightning Source LLC
Chambersburg PA
CBHW070427010526
44118CB00014B/1940